THE CAMPBELTOWN & MACHRIHANISH
LIGHT RAILWAY

'Argyll' and train at Machrihanish, 1906 (F. Moore)

THE CAMPBELTOWN & MACHRIHANISH LIGHT RAILWAY

by

NIGEL S. C. MACMILLAN
C Eng, MI Mech E

Illustrated by Fraser Cameron

DAVID & CHARLES : NEWTON ABBOT

ISBN 0 7153 4919 8

Set in eleven point Pilgrim
and printed in Great Britain
by Bristol Typesetting Company Limited
for David & Charles (Publishers) Limited
South Devon House Newton Abbot Devon

Contents

APPENDIXES

List of Illustrations

IN THE TEXT

APPENDIX I

Introduction

During the early 1930s, a wee boy in a Macmillan kilt was playing around Campbeltown harbour. Like all boys, fishing boats and harbours had a magnetic attraction, but this harbour had something even more interesting—rails. True, they only ran along one of the two piers and were truncated as they curved off the shore end. Even at that age, the rails seemed strangely close together to the boy. What could have run on them? The wee boy was the author and such was his first introduction to the Campbeltown & Machrihanish Light Railway which was to dominate much of his later life. He was accompanying his father on a business trip and had not come, as most people did, by boat, but round the long winding road, single track in many places, that tried the old Morris Cowley sorely.

Campbeltown, Tarbert and Oban all have similar harbours and for a while confusion raged in the boy's mind as to which had had the rails. But then there were more important things for a growing boy to think of—A4s, Scots, Hornbys and the new Coronations.

His next time in Campbeltown was again accompanying his father on business. By now Campbeltown was a restricted area (1941) and the business was the Clyde defences. The rails on the New Quay had gone but the more experienced eye of a senior school boy spotted the cutting and the road-bed was explored from end to end. At the top of the cutting, the still embedded sleepers had unexplained ironwork fastened to them (still unexplained in 1969 but probably point locking gear) and surely this was a half-filled-in inspection pit? The butts of the shooting range were built of small sleepers with dog-spikes but there was a war on and few people had the time or the inclination to talk.

On the other side of the Campbeltown Loch, behind the barbed wire and the naval sentry, were some American looking carriage bodies, but even to look through the wire was to court suspicion.

What railway had this been in the far corner of Kintyre? What engines ran on it no one seemed to know.

During the early 1950s, there was an upsurge in interest in light and narrow gauge railways, as these died off one by one. Starting with the Talyllyn, some were saved by preservation societies and now flourish, but at that time the interest was relatively new. Articles on both full size and model narrow gauge subjects were plentiful but were strangely silent about the Campbeltown Railway.

The author decided that he had had enough of Compounds and Dunalastairs for the time being, and would build a model of the C & M train to show the Sassenachs and Welshmen that Scotland too had had a narrow gauge line as fine as anything in the south.

And that is how it started. To build an engine, one needs drawings. The builders' drawings require redrawing to the scale of the model. Photographs are necessary for the fine detail. In 1954 the author had the good fortune to get married and the even greater fortune to have his bride cheerfully trek the route from Campbeltown to Machrihanish on their honeymoon and pose by the Chiscan bridge. Gradually the information built up until now most of the story is available. This book is the logical conclusion to the project.

The author has now built models of all the C & M engines, carriages and wagons, and three models of the actual railway at Campbeltown; the harbour, the cutting and the sheds, each model bigger than its predecessor, so that now the 'wee train' can be seen again in Hall Street, if only in miniature.

NSCM
'Dunalastair'
1969.

CHAPTER ONE

The Kintyre Peninsula

The Kintyre Peninsula is situated at the southern end of western Scotland. The area should not be confused with that known as south-west Scotland from which it is separated by the lower reaches of the Firth of Clyde. Kintyre comprises a long neck of mountainous country forty miles long and eight miles wide. It was very nearly one of the Western Isles, and in Roman times was described as an island. At the northern end, the land mass is nipped at Tarbert by two arms of the sea leaving only a mile wide isthmus. Again ten miles from its southern end, a geological fault has caused a section of the land to sink and the sea has flooded in to form the natural harbour now known as Campbeltown Loch.

The remoteness of the land has resulted in its dependency from classical times on sea-borne transport. Until the ninth century AD, the Scots had their capital at the southern end. The older alternative name for the district, *Dalriada* is derived from the name of the first Celtic king who settled there.

During the Norse occupation of the Western Isles, the possession of Dalriada was fiercely disputed. In 1093, Magnus the Barefoot, a Viking chief, was granted all the lands round which a boat could sail. The wily Magnus had his galley with sail set, drawn across the isthmus at Tarbert, while he stood at the helm, and claimed Kintyre as his own. The name Tarbert is believed to be derived from *Tarruing*, to draw, and *Buta*, a boat. Thus Kintyre came under Norse rule and remained so until the Vikings were defeated at the Battle of Renfrew on the upper Clyde in 1164. For a time, after the seat of government had been transferred to the mainland, the area was ruled by a branch of the Clan Macdonald who became sufficiently strong to defy the throne. James IV found it necessary to land in Kintyre and evict the Macdonalds from their stronghold. This done he left a garrison to maintain the royal authority. But Macdonald was neither daunted nor intimidated and before the king's ships were clear of the harbour, the castle was retaken and the governor hanged from the wall before the king's eyes.

The government of the day thought it expedient to arrange for one local tribe to subdue the other. Accordingly the Lordship of Kintyre was taken from Macdonald and transferred to the family of Argyll who at last succeeded in gaining the upper hand, and have held the land to the present day.

In 1609 Archibald Campbell, the 7th Earl, built a castle at Kilkerran near the head of the loch and gave his name to the small settlement that grew up round the fortress. Known as Gilleaspuig Gruamach (Archibald the Grim) he also founded the Campbeltown whisky industry, by granting a licence to John Boyll of Kelburn to distil aqua vitae. The town, however, is considered to date from 1700 when a royal charter was granted to the tenth Earl of Argyll.

Campbeltown owes its existence to being situated at one end of a perfect natural harbour. Campbeltown Loch is about two miles long and a mile wide. The entrance from the Kilbrennan Sound is almost closed by Davaar Island. In sailing days the town traded with the West Indies, Virginia and the Baltic for rum, tobacco and timber. In the eighteenth century the voyage to Glasgow could take many days, but the introduction of steam navigation reduced the journey to hours. The first steamer to call was the seventy-three ton *Brittania* (sic) in 1816 under the flag of McLellan & Laird. Very soon there was a thrice fortnightly service to Glasgow and a weekly sailing to Londonderry. In 1826 the Campbeltown & Carradale Steam Packet Joint Stock Co was formed. Their early ships rejoiced in names like *Gael*, *Druid*, *Celt*, *St Kiaran*, and oddly *Duke of Cornwall* and *Duke of Lancaster*. Their last ships, *Davaar*, *Dalriada*, *Kintyre* and *Kinloch* are still remembered by many on the Clyde. During the nineteenth century, the Clyde paddle steamers were in their heyday, but in 1902 there started running to Campbeltown from Glasgow two new turbine steamers, *Queen Alexandra* and *King Edward*. These vessels and their successors made the return trip daily and brought Campbel-

town within day tripper range. Since the middle of the
twentieth century the position of sea travel has declined and
now most goods and travellers come by road or air even
though the road takes 140 miles to cover 60 miles as the crow
flies.

ss *Davaar*, bowsprit and figurehead

Fishing has always been an important industry and the town
still supports a large fishing fleet. In 240 AD, Polinus described
the inhabitants as living principally on milk and fish. Herring
were reported to be plentiful in the area in 1447, and in 1630,
120 sailing vessels were based in Campbeltown. The industry
received a boost by the payment of a bounty in 1750 to all

fishing boats over twenty tons and this was granted to smaller boats in 1787. By the time the bounty was withdrawn in 1800 herring fishing was firmly established. Ring netting started in Loch Fyne in 1833 and despite bitter opposition became universally accepted even before it was legalised. The Loch Fyne fishing boat was most distinctive and survived until recent years. It had a sloping canoe stern with an external rudder and a steeply raked mast on which was carried a standing lug sail. The first petrol paraffin engine was fitted to one in 1910 to become the predecessor of the present fleet of some thirty-five diesel vessels.

Shipbuilding has also concerned Campbeltown and in the 1830s coastal schooners were being built where the railway terminus was later sited. In 1877 a yard was opened on the opposite side of the loch at Trench Point where the first ship to be built was a 100 ton schooner, *May*, which was 84 ft long. She was an unlucky ship for after several Atlantic crossings she was sunk off Davaar Island in 1883 with the loss of all hands. In over half a century of building, 151,000 tons of shipping were produced, the largest vessel being *Roquelle* of 4,363 tons in 1918. The last was *Akenside* in 1922. (A new ship-yard has recently been built at Trench Point and it is to be hoped that Campbeltown-built vessels will soon be seen again.) At Trench Point the Campbeltown railway's carriages ended their days as holiday huts.

'Campbeltown Loch, I wish you were whisky' and it very nearly was. During the last century there were thirty-five distilleries in Campbeltown. Now there are two. Distilling began in the early seventeenth century and brewing in 1770. In those days the illicit distilling of whisky and smuggling of other spirits was completely out of official control and to combat this the government of the day banned all stills in the Highlands under 500 gallons. This boost to large producers was the start of the modern industry in Campbeltown and the first big plant was opened by John Beith & Co in 1817.

Modern Campbeltown is a burgh with a population of some 6,500 and is adapting itself well to the changing industrial demands of the present day. Although coal mining has stopped and distilling declined, it is still the economic centre of the neighbourhood. While not on the main tourist trail in Scotland,

Page 17 (above) *View of Campbeltown from Barley Bannocks Hill showing Colliery Railway and Rifle Range;* (below) *0–4–2ST* Chevalier *on train of early hutch carriers*

Page 18 (above) *Passenger train at harbour before commencement of service. Note, no crane on New Quay;* (centre) *Cutting the cutting;* (below) *the new service*

the district nevertheless attracts an increasing number of holidaymakers with its pleasant scenery and beaches.

At the other side of the peninsula lies the village of Machrihanish. Situated at the end of a glorious beach and backed by rocky cliffs, the village was formerly known as Mary Pans or Salt Pans, the old name having been derived from the evaporation of sea water to obtain salt. In the past, despite the dangerous shore and the absence of a safe harbour, fishing was the staple industry, particularly for lobsters and cod and a lifeboat was maintained until the mid 1920s.

At the beginning of this century, the character of the village changed with the building of several residential villas, and by the development of excellent golf links. Summer visitors started to appear in large numbers and the English language ousted the Gaelic as the local people catered more and more for the tourists. In 1905 the National Electric Signalling Company of Pittsburgh USA built a 425 ft wireless telegraphy mast. Its purpose was the transatlantic transmission of radio messages and the entire project was heavily clothed in secrecy. Locally the personnel were regarded as foreign spies. Tests came to an abrupt end the following year when the whole erection came crashing down in a storm. The enormous mooring pads of the guys supporting the structure bear mute witness of its size to this day. (An early picture of the train shows the mast in the background.)

CHAPTER TWO

Campbeltown Coalfield

ENVIRONMENTAL DESCRIPTION

The peninsula of Kintyre, in most parts mountainous in character, is divided transversely towards its southern end by a low-lying plain known as the Laggan. It terminates on the east side at Campbeltown Loch, and on the west at Machrihanish Bay. Its general elevation does not exceed 50 or 60 feet above sea level. Both north and south the ground rises abruptly into hills over 1,000 feet in height, composed of ancient metamorphic rocks. Within the area thus defined lies Campbeltown coalfield. It extends under the sea at Machrihanish Bay, but is cut off towards Campbeltown by the outcrop of the underlying rocks of the old red sandstone. Although the Campbeltown coalfield is detached from the other coalfields of Scotland it is of the same geological age, and forms part of that strip of carboniferous strata which, with certain interruptions, extends from the east of Scotland to the Antrim coast.

The limits of the coalfield are not precisely determined. Not only does it extend under the sea on the west side, as already stated, for a distance at present unknown, but its northern boundary is also to some extent uncertain. The greater part of the Laggan has a thick covering of peat, gravel, and other superficial deposits which conceal the rocks beneath and obscure the line of demarcation which separates the coal measures from the older strata upon which they repose. (Further details of the coal deposits can be found in Appendix 4.)

EARLY COAL WINNING

The working of this coal has a spasmodic and chequered

history, but can be dated back to the fifteenth century. In 1494, James IV of Scotland visited Tarbert, Dunaverty and Kilkerran. Shortly afterwards on 27 April 1498 there is an entry in the accounts of the Lord High Treasurer of Scotland of 18s to a 'cole man' to go to Kintyre to see if coals may be won there. A further entry on 5 May in the same year itemises to one Davidson, 'colzar' to make tools and proceed to Kintyre for a further 18s, and four days later 3s were paid to the 'colzar' in Dumbarton when he embarked by sea. From these references, it would appear that James IV may himself have instigated the survey.

In 1633 James Campbell, Lord Kintyre, granted a feu charter to Archibald McDonald of Sanda and when this feu was re-disponed in 1669 by Archibald Campbell, the 9th Earl, to Ronald McDonald of Sanda, the Earl reserved to himself 'all mines, minerals, coals and coal heughs' that shall be found there, but added that it would be lawful for McDonald to win coal for his own use. From this early date the Dukes of Argyll encouraged coal working in the area. However, the mineral rights did the 9th Earl but little good because by an act of James VII (James II of England) all the Earl's lands were forfeited when he was executed in 1685. It was not until William and Mary were on the throne that Argyllshire was restored to Campbell.

Meanwhile coal was being worked and was used to evaporate brine on the coast at a spot known still as Mary Pans or Salt Pans and situated in the modern village of Machrihanish. Baptismal records of the 1670s and 80s refer to children born to 'John Maxwell, coal carrier' and 'Hugh Kirkland, oversman'.

Coal was still being worked in 1701 but by 1706 a petition was raised by Elizabeth, Duchess of Argyll, regarding the life rent of the coal heughs which had fallen into ruins. Following the Duchess's death in 1735 coal was again wrought until 1743 when work was abandoned due to the coal being of poor quality and the salt pans and surrounding property again became ruinous.

In the summer of 1745 a survey was made and it was decided that coal could indeed be wrought provided that a steam engine or windmill was built to pump the working clear. Eight men were employed for a fortnight sinking a shaft

which went down 18 or 20 ft until they came on a bed of running sand. No matter how they cleared it with buckets during
the day it was full again the next morning. The outbreak of
the 45 Rebellion effectively put an end to any further work.

Mining got under way again in 1747 but in 1749 there were
complaints that the workings were too near the surface and
that the roof was so bad as to be dangerous. The deepest
galleries were four fathoms below the surface and the shallow-
est only two. The small coal was used at the Salt Pans about a
mile from the pit and the large coal was carted to Campbeltown. Work at this period fell off during the winter as the
carriage of the coal became virtually impossible and at Salt
Pans, rain water constantly diluted the brine.

In 1752 a report was made to His Grace, the Duke of Argyll,
that there was a 'large body of coalls extant in the grounds of
Drumlemill' and that the seam was 6 ft 6 in thick. Three new
borings between Drumlemble and the sea had shown that this
seam was considerable but dropped 27 ft towards the sea. To
prevent flooding a horse gin or water-driven pump was
proposed but it was added that these would only keep the
working free from water in the summertime. Another seam
was known to exist at a deeper level but was considered
impossible to work because of the added pumping difficulties
commensurate with its depth. At this time the harbour at
Campbeltown was considered much better for exporting coal
than those at Saltcoats, Irvine or Ayr.

In 1773 coal was once more being worked and taken by
pack pony or cart to Campbeltown. But transport was a major
problem and because of the almost complete lack of a proper
road, the new mineowner Charles McDowell arranged for
James Watt of steam fame to survey the route for a canal
between his pit and Campbeltown. Transport to the sea in the
west was no easier but it was only a quarter of the distance.
Loading was hazardous on the exposed coast. It was made even
more so in 1774 when the Customs Surveyor seized an open
boat carrying 2 tons of coal, while it lay at Ardpatrick. The
coal had been loaded at Mary Pans (Machrihanish) and the
owner claimed ignorance of the necessity to have a customs
house docket. McDowell now turned his attention to improv-
ing transport to Campbeltown and started to cut his canal in

1785. The Campbeltown town council immediately took out an interdict to prevent him building his canal next to the Mill Dam. The following year various tenants in Drumlemble jumped on the band wagon and sued McDowell for damages to land and property caused by the coalworks.

However this storm was weathered and the pit prospered under J. Christie, the now ailing McDowell's overseer, and the output for the years 1788-91 was 31,418, 40,987 and 34,937 loads respectively (a load was ⅓ ton). McDowell died on 11 September 1791.

The Muniments of Argyll at Inveraray Castle reveals that the inhabitants of the Duke of Argyll's estate in the area at that time were: —

	Men	Women	Children	Total
Coalhill	39	41	63	143
Drumlemble	26	34	26	86
Ballygreggan Dalquhason Mary Pans	17	24	29	70
	82	99	118	299

John Christie was still working the pit in 1797 when the persons supplying the horses refused to do so any longer as they considered they had been unfairly treated. It was necessary for Christie to get the Duke's Chamberlain to intervene and settle the dispute. The pit had been idle for six weeks as a result of a broken beam on the pit engine and a replacement had to be obtained from Greenock. Greenock is today only a few hours sail from Campbeltown, but to transport an enormous piece of machinery like this by sailing coaster to Campbeltown and thence by canal must have been a tremendous undertaking.

It was the practice at this period for the colliers to have some farm land where they could keep cows and graze their horses (presumably pit ponies) and there was a constant bickering between the coal company and the local tenant farmers as to how much land should be thus used.

At the end of the eighteenth century, the canal was being used to transport some 4,500 tons of coal per year to Campbeltown for local use in three flat-bottom barges. These must have been quite small as their capital value was only £69 for all three. In contrast a water wheel in use at the colliery was valued at £169. In addition shipment to Ireland and elsewhere was developing and the sloops *Susanna* and *Favorite* (sic) are mentioned in this connection.

Despite a steady production of coal through the turn of the century, the company found increasing maintenance costs made things very difficult and had to appeal frequently to the Duke to be excused from paying royalties etc. The farmers along the canal route were forever claiming damages from neglected bridges and aqueducts. The coal company sank two new shafts in 1804, unfortunately in the wrong place. Water was a constant nuisance and the cost of pumping added to the company's financial worries. The steam engine employed at this time had a 34 in dia cylinder and a 14 ft diameter boiler: it was working 10 in dia pumps in the mine at a depth of 20 fathoms. In 1807 the company successfully prevailed upon the Duke to forbid the cutting of peat to help promote coal sales. In the same year an unexpected source of income came when the Swedish ship *Lars Johan* was wrecked on the beach at Machrihanish. The mine manager Mr Hogg bought the wreck for £450 of which the Duke paid £60.

For the next 25 years, the coalworks ran fairly well with an annual output of 10,000 to 15,000 tons. In February 1835 the pit became flooded. It was not cleared till June the following year and was no sooner working again when the miners went on strike. They demanded to be paid on gross output and apparently were successful in their claim.

In 1837 a new pit was opened 627 yd from the canal terminus and a similar distance from the main road. To transport the coal from the pit head to the coal depot at the canal a tramroad was built. This must represent a record in various forms of transport over so short a distance: to cover $4\frac{1}{2}$ miles, the coal travelled by rail, canal, horse drawn cart and was finally discharged into coastal shipping.

In 1841, John Howie, a competent manager for many years, died and the company was thrown into confusion. Coal continued to be extracted from a 7 ft seam but in 1847 several faults were struck. A new pit was sunk but hard rock prevented its reaching the coal and several unsuccessful trial bores were made. In desperation to keep the pit going, a mine was dug from the main shaft for the removal of the pillars. In so doing a 3 ft 8 in seam was struck by accident, and longwall* working started. This is one of the few instances of longwall working being employed in this coalfield.

In 1851, a clay mill near Lochsannish farm closed down depriving the coal company of a nearby market. In the same year coal extraction commenced in a seam known as the Parrot seam. The quality was not of the best and production for the year hovered around the 15,000 ton mark. Much of it was used by the Campbeltown distillers but coal from Hurlford near Kilmarnock in Ayrshire was imported in this year.

The working of the Parrot seam did not last long and by 1855 the pit was reduced to a care and maintenance basis when the lease for the tenancy ran out. The Duke took immediate steps to have the canal filled in. The poor state of repair of the earthworks had caused it to be a constant nuisance to tenants of adjoining ground and weeds and silting had made navigation difficult. In 1861 the pumps, underground rails, and engine were brought up and the mine closed. The assembled machinery was sold off at Drumlemble two years later.

THE RAILWAY ERA

Spasmodic coal working continued over the next few years with mention of pits at Kilkivan and Trodigal and elsewhere but the major step forward came in 1875 when the Argyll

---

* In LONGWALL working, a method of extraction is employed where a tunnel is driven through the coal seam, ie, it will initially have coal as both side walls and a ceiling and floor of rock. The roof will be shored up. Coal will be taken from one wall and as the tunnel widens the roof supports are withdrawn at the back and transferred nearer the working face. The abandoned part is either packed with spoil or allowed to collapse.

In STOUP & ROOM working (also known as Pillar & Room, Stoup & Stool, etc) a tunnel is driven as before but further tunnels are cut into the faces on one or both sides at right angles to the initial one. These are usually four times the seam thickness apart. As these tunnels progress, further tunnels are driven parallel to the first one until a giant lattice is developed whereby 75 per cent of the coal seam is left in large pillars to support the terrain above. This method goes back to antiquity but is seldom used now.

Coal & Cannel* Co Ltd was formed. A lease was taken from the Duke of Argyll for thirty-one years. In its prospectus, the Argyll Coal & Cannel Co mentioned known seams 2 ft, 6 ft, 9 ft, and 6 ft thick, holding 20,000,000 tons. As cartage would cost 2s 6d per ton an agreement was signed with the Duke to solve the transport problem by building a railway from the colliery to Campbeltown which would reduce cartage to 6d per ton. It pointed out that Campbeltown had 8,000 inhabitants and 20 distilleries consuming 600 tons of coal per week. Furthermore, boats bringing barley from France for the whisky making could load coal for the return trip. The new shaft was sunk at Drumlemble on Kilkivan farm in May 1876.

Coal mining got off to a flying start and was helped by the new steam-worked narrow gauge railway being able to deliver it quickly to the new depot at the coal ree in Argyll Street. In 1878 while coal was being worked at 27 fathoms, old workings full of water were broken into. A rough dam backed by boulders was built to retain the water and all went well until 5 July when the manager noted mud and water flowing from the dam. Further strengthening took place but on the afternoon of the following day, the water found its way round the dam by way of a fault in the strata and the sudden flood completely overwhelmed the workings. Fortunately work was nearly over for the day but the bottomer and two miners were drowned, another five escaping through other shafts. It was not until 2 September that the pumps were able to clear the mine and the bodies of the unfortunate miners retrieved.

House coal was being sold at this time at 6s 8d per ton and bagged cwts at 6d each! Coal was being exported to Norway, Sweden, Prussia and Denmark, the schooner *Julie* being mentioned in this context.

In 1881 a new pit was sunk half a mile to the west. The new pit was later named Wimbledon after a local man had won the Wimbledon shooting competition. The railway was extended to the new pit-head. Coal was struck in June 1881. In September the administration of the Argyll c & c c passed into the hands of J. & L. Galloway whose energy proved the mainspring of developments of both the mine and the various railway activities over the next thirty-five years.

* Cannel is a hard coal, rich in oil and gas.

Argyll Colliery, 1900

In 1897 the Campbeltown Coal Co was formed to take over the Argyll colliery and the lease from the Duke extended for a further thirty years. The seam worked at this time was the 9 ft one mentioned earlier.

Of the Galloway family, T. Lindsay Galloway was a resourceful and clever engineer. By 1902 the colliery had two shafts, No 1 was 5 ft 6 in by 11 ft 6 in and No 2 was 5 ft 6 in by 8 ft 6 in. The steam winding engine had a single cylinder 20 in dia by 4 ft 6 in stroke. A compressor provided power for underground haulage equipment hauling rakes of 10-12 hutches. The coal output steadily increased from 10,483 tons in 1897 to 25,610 tons in 1903.

In 1905 electricity was introduced and coal mining was proceeding under the sea. This under-sea coal was an annoyance to the Duke as there was no royalty paid on it as the lease was from the Crown. He insisted that at least half the coal used in the pit boilers should be got from his property. In the following year screens and a new head gear were erected as the earlier one had only lifted the hutches high enough to be run on to the flat railway wagons.

The war years 1914-18 proved difficult for the company. Nearly one third of the employees had been called to the colours and although the demand for coal was great, the difficulty of producing it was greater. During the war, sandstone was brought up from the mine. It was of a quality particularly suitable for glassmaking being completely free from iron contamination. T. L. Galloway made investigations to see if a bottle factory could be started locally but it was found more economic to ship the sand elsewhere. In 1917 the first of a series of new names made its appearance, the Kintyre Coal & Oil Co Ltd. The Galloways retired in 1918 by selling their shares in the C C C. The poor old C C C now entered a period of speculative intrigue from which it never recovered. The Duke's tenant of the coalfield was the Campbeltown Coal Co but the controlling owners of the company's shares changed hands at a pace so fast and furious that His Grace had great difficulty in keeping track of who in fact was responsible. Matters came to a head in 1921 when one of the directors, J. Stoner, described as an Austrian Jew, withdrew the company's liquid assets from its London bank and fled the country. In the same year there was a strike of miners and the entire workings were flooded. This was particularly disastrous as the undersea coal seam could not be cleared of water and was abandoned. This effectively prevented any further extension westward. In 1925 a fire at the pit bottom caused the main workings to be abandoned also.

The lease terminated in 1927 and Walkers & Kimber became the new tenants. Coal production was surprisingly good this year, totalling 25,000 tons, and 79 miners were employed. Most of the coal was taken from around the pit bottom, but only those directly concerned knew this. In June the following year the Franco British Co acquired the Argyll colliery and at a Campbeltown Town Council meeting on 13 August, Mr Maisel, a director, asked that gas be got from the proposed distillation plant and bought by the town. At the same time, a report to the shareholders states that a testing plant of the Aicher low temperature carbonisation process had been in operation for a fortnight, under the supervision of Mr Aicher. Tests gave yields of between $34\frac{1}{2}$ and 74 gallons of crude oil per ton of coal. In addition 2,350 cubic ft/ton of gas and the residual coke were available from the process.

In June 1929 the Franco British Company re-emerged as the Coal Carbonisation Trust and their prospectus mentioned carbonising 1,000 tons of coal per day yielding 11 cwt of coke per ton.

Almost immediately afterwards the pit at Kilkivan was abandoned and the whole project 'melted like snow off a dyke'.

Three years later the coal company's activities were wound up for the last time.

RECENT WORKING

This account of the coal mining in Kintyre would not be complete without discussing the re-opening of the colliery following the second world war. In 1943 the Glasgow Iron & Steel Co began boring and on the success of this, two drifts were driven in 1946. The new colliery was officially opened in May of that year by Lady Lithgow, wife of Sir James Lithgow. At the same time the National Government was considering open-cast mining but thought better of it.

In July 1947 the mine was nationalised and came under the N C B Central West Area administered from Glasgow, Mr John Williamson being appointed manager. At this time, the main mine descended from the surface for 150 yards at a gradient of 1 in 4 and the companion mine 103 yards at 1 in 2.5. By September 25 tons per day were being brought up. There was no longer any question of the poor Machrihanish coal competing with the Ayrshire brand. Consumers were told by the N C B they would take Kintyre coal or nothing. (This edict was subsequently relaxed.) Messrs J. B. Brodie & Co of Glasgow surveyed a route between Machrihanish and Campbeltown for a standard gauge railway or possibly an aerial ropeway and there was hope that the old line would be resurrected but the coal board decided to buy a fleet of 10 tipper lorries. Screening plant at the colliery came from Broomside Colliery and the new loading plant at the old quay was made up from spare equipment at Cowdenbeath.

It is ironical to note that in December 1949 the old coal bing of earlier days was on fire and oil was being distilled from the coal by the process, and oozing out at the foot of it.

In 1950 the first shipment of coal to Belfast took place when 270 tons of dross were loaded on *Tannamore*. The following month *Transig* took on bunkers. Soon after *Corteen* loaded 537 tons of dross and 15 tons of bunker coal.

That summer the miners went on strike all over Scotland but Argyll colliery restarted the following week in advance of the other pits.

Coal was stocked in Glebe Street, Campbeltown, so as to be on hand when boats called to load. This was unpopular with the householders nearby as the dust caused a great nuisance. Shipment to Ireland during 1951 averaged about 1,500 to 1,800 tons per week. In this year the pithead baths were started and a mine rescue service organised whereby specialists from Coatbridge could be flown in from Renfrew in an emergency.

By February in the following year 141,620 tons had been shipped and three boats per week were calling. Output was 500 tons per day. April found the Dutch coaster *Nelly* loading 700 tons of domestic coal for Rotterdam and another Dutchman *Carpo* loading 660 tons for Copenhagen and 550 tons for

Ballylumford. This was the best week in Kintyre's history, 3,000 tons loaded, half of it to Holland.

In 1954 Mr Williamson left and was succeeded by Mr Thom. Production for these years makes interesting comparisons with earlier days:

	Production in tons	Percentage shipped
1950	65,236	77.5
1951	100,033	79.7
1952	90,032	77.9
1953	84,530	80.4

In 1954 Mr Thom arranged for the author to make a visit underground. The surprising thing about the coalfield was that it lay on a 1 in 4 gradient in line with the entry shaft. Anywhere one went underground one either went down 1 in 4 or up 1 in 4. The 'rooms' were tunnels 14 ft wide and 10 ft high and supported when in use by 12 ft x 4 in x 4 in H girders on wooden props. About 260 men were employed at the time. Underground, only officials (and visitors) had electric lamps: the miners themselves had open carbide lamps. This had an amusing sequel. When a face was about to be blasted, the miners all retired round the corner of the next pillar to await the blast. When it came, it blew all the lamps out. There were flints for lighting the lamps but as soon as one lamp was lit, the men all solemnly touched foreheads to relight their individual lamps.

The coal was loaded on to shaking conveyers and 'shoogled' down to the lowest gallery and thence along a belt conveyer to the main drift where a further belt conveyer took it to the surface. The seam being worked at this time was said to be 15 ft thick although only the middle 10 ft was being taken out. The history of water troubles was apparent as pumps were producing 500 gallons per minute on the surface although the mine galleries were quite dry. The stock pile had just recently been moved to the colliery itself.

The output for January to October 1954 was 79,615 tons and for the same period in 1955, 77,528 tons. The total amount shipped to this date was 560,801 tons.

In 1956, Mr Thom left and was succeeded by Mr D. M. Seaman.

The mine was much deeper than any of the earlier ones and was much further from the colliery buildings than early haulage systems would have allowed. The main shaft went down at an angle for three quarters of a mile to 125 fathoms. As the workings spread out ventilation became a problem and good galleries which had been cleared in 1951 were utilised for the return air circuit. In 1958 spontaneous combustion ignited the coal near the return airways and a serious fire developed. Dousing it was quite ineffectual and as the fire was high up the return slope, flooding could only be resorted to after four seals had been built to contain the water. New airways were subsequently driven through stone to prevent any recurrence of the problem. Two months' production were lost but on 25 November limited working of main coal was resumed.

In 1959 the Coras Iompair Eireann (Irish State Railway) was being converted to diesel traction and its orders for coal ceased in March. To reduce costs and increase output selected stoops were withdrawn, as had been done thirty-five years earlier. Whether as a direct result of this or not, severe crushing started on the main roadways the following year and all workings more than 200 yards from the mine foot were abandoned. As heating was detected the old galleries were allowed to flood. Two stone drifts were driven through the stone of West Parkfergus fault to seek fresh coal but there seemed to be more faults than coal there. The manpower was being reduced as each development produced new faults and worse still, more water.

In 1964 the main and mid-coal seams were given up and work concentrated in the Kilkivan seam but the coal was poor and the markets were shrinking. On 26 March 1967, production ceased. Underground salvage work continued till June and the unwanted surface buildings demolished. The baths, garage, workshops, sub station, and office were left for use in developing the area as a caravan and camping site.

The scale of working in the final years was as follows:

	Men employed	Output (tons)	Tonnage shipped
1956	263	101,815	84,801
1957	267	99,775	91,469
1958	273	75,377	69,254
1959	280	81,320	66,946

1960	200	34,186	21,461
1961	150	28,000	24,000
1962	140	46,565	40,000
1963	120	30,718	
1964	115	31,300	
1965	100	40,000	
1966	80	40,000	

So the coalworks have finally closed, not because the coal is worked out, but because mining it for a dwindling and competitive market is no longer economic.

CHAPTER THREE

The Colliery Railway

In the middle of the nineteenth century a new railway development appeared. The Festiniog railway in Wales, a horse and
gravity operated tramway, in 1863 successfully harnessed
steam power to its narrow track gauge of 1 ft 11¾ in. Following this achievement many industrial railways were built
employing gauges of similar dimensions, but steam worked
from their inception. As land transport was primitive and
subject to seasonal variation, and the canal was now moribund
as we have seen in the preceding chapter, the new techno-
logical advance of a steam narrow gauge railway was grasped
by the coal company as a solution to its problem.

The western terminus of the canal was at Drumlemble
village between West Drumlemble farm and the main road.
There was a coal depot here and latterly a wagon tramway
ran north west to the later pit. The canal headed ENE until
level with Bleachfield and then curved round in a big S bend
to cross the Chiscan Water at Lintmill, the bridge abutments
still being visible. A further curve took it almost due north past
North Moy farm. About a mile from Campbeltown it turned
east again and followed the south bank of the mill lade until
abreast of the mill dam when it turned almost due south to the
old coal ree. From here, coal was carted to domestic consumers, distilleries and to the harbour for shipment.

Many written sources claim that when the canal was filled
in the railway was built on its course. Apart from a few
hundred yards near Bleachfield this is definitely not so. If
indeed the railway had followed the canal it would have saved
much heart searching later on because the route chosen
involved a steep climb in both directions over the ridge at
Tomaig near Campbeltown. The colliery railway perpetuated

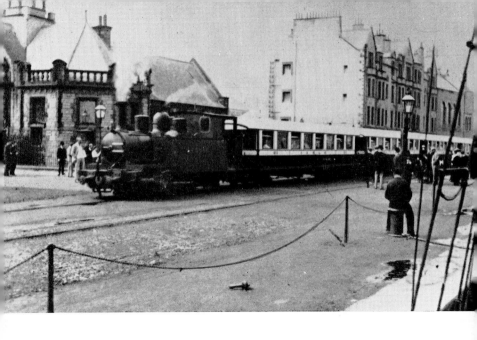

Page 35 *Scenes in Hall Street 1906, 1929.* (above) Argyll *chuffs past the free library;* (below) *Wee McCabe has a word with the driver*

Page 36 (above) Argyll *on the Steamer express, note the missing stone ball on the Christian Institute;* (below) *New Quay showing coal crane*

Page 37 (above) *Armistice in the rain 1918. The procession passes the passenger train in Hall Street;* (below) *Quarry Green. A rare view of an engine facing Campbeltown. Coach No 6 at rear is just clearing the Kilkerran Road crossing*

Page 38 (above) *Golfers express emerging from the cutting at Limecraigs 1906. Site of later carriage shed behind locomotive* Argyll; *(below) nearing Machrihanish, 1906. The colliery is in background and the train is just about to cross the main Campbeltown to Machrihanish road*

the canal's failing of terminating in the centre of Campbeltown thus necessitating a double transhipment if the coal were to be loaded aboard ship. It is difficult to see why this short-sighted policy prevailed especially as in 1876 the town was not nearly so built up along the sea front as it was when the line eventually came to the harbour in 1906.

The building of the railway started in 1876 on a light formation composed of tipped coal slag and the right of way was by private arrangement with the Duke of Argyll who in effect owned the trackbed. At one stage the Duke laid claim to the rails and sleepers as well, but the coal company's solicitors were able to obtain an amicable settlement. The sleepers for the railway arrived from St Malo on *Levonia* on 2 September 1876. The engine *Pioneer* arrived on the steamer *Kintyre* on 11 November. The first run by the engine was on Christmas day which in Scotland in those days would be a normal working day (and continued to be so until about 1960). On 21 April the following year the railway was completed although the wagons were still awaited from Glasgow. At a Board of Trade enquiry on 1 November, there was opposition to the railway from Captain Stewart, a local landowner.

The railway originally started at the Kilkivan Pit, about $4\frac{1}{4}$ miles from Campbeltown, but in 1881 it was extended westward to the new colliery making the total distance 4.7 miles. The 21 ft iron rails were 30 lb per yard and were flat bottomed. They were spiked direct to wooden sleepers at 3 ft centres. The speed on the line was about 15 mph and even with the 9 ton *Pioneer* the rails soon became badly bent, especially at the rail joints. Once sleepers started to rot and fishplates worked slack things got very bad indeed. The bigger *Chevalier* caused even more damage and eventually both locomotives were converted to the 0–4–2 wheel arrangement by the addition of a trailing truck. A policy of using larger sleepers 4 ft 6 in by 9 in by $4\frac{1}{2}$ in was instigated and nine were used where previously there had been seven. Closer spacing was employed at the rail joints. In addition all new work and repairs were carried out using steel 40 lb rail which gave no trouble.

The railway ran due east out of the new colliery but after crossing the West Machrihanish farm road began to curve to the right towards the site of the earlier pits. At Drumlemble it

c

again headed due west until it met the bed of the old canal, filled in about fifteen years prior to the railway being opened. This course was only followed for a few hundred yards until the canal route curves off to the right while the railway went straight on. The Chiscan water was crossed by a bridge consisting of two I beams with a deck of standard gauge railway sleepers. Immediately after this bridge, the Aros Road was crossed on the level. The line proceeded generally eastwards to Plantation, crossing the canal bed at right angles on the way. At Plantation where the main Campbeltown to Southend road was crossed, there was a sharp bend of 150 ft radius to the right where the wheels screeved badly. Shortly after this the route begins to climb to Tomaig. Once over this ridge, the railway plummeted down towards Campbeltown, across the rifle range between the 400 yd and 500 yd butts(!) and curved round to the left. It then entered a stone-lined cutting in which there was an iron gate; past the Highland Parish (Gaelic) Church and emerged at the coal ree at the end of Argyll Street.

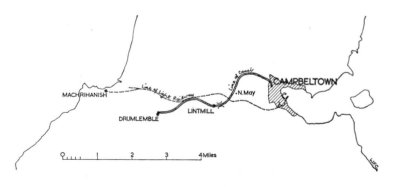

ROUTE OF COLLIERY CANAL

T. Lindsay Galloway, the colliery engineer, was greatly troubled latterly by the combined effects of the sharp curve at Plantation crossing and the steep climb up to Tomaig in both directions. The former limited him to 4-coupled engines which were really too small for the hill. Thus these apparently trifling errors were able to mar the whole design. It matters not how level or how straight a railway may be for the greater part of its length; one bad gradient or one sharp curve will restrict the capacity of the whole line.

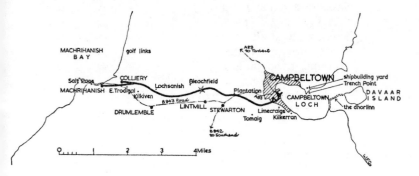

ROUTE OF LIGHT RAILWAY

There were a number of level crossings on the line, the most important one being at Plantation. This crossing was also known to the local people as the 'Hungry Hoose'. At one time there was a public house here and of all the hostelries between Campbeltown and the west coast only this one served no bannocks with a dram, hence the name. Plantation crossing was protected by gates and the crossing keeper was a woman who tenanted a cottage nearby which was owned by the railway. In the colliery railway days there was a signal to protect the crossing. The other crossings had gates also but these were later discarded in favour of cross trenches to prevent sheep and cattle from straying on to the line. They were of dubious value as animals tended to fall into the pit and be unable to get out. On one occasion the train was held up all night until a horse was extracted. Gates embarrassed the railway in other ways; shortly after delivery, *Princess* crushed a man to death against the gate in the old stone cutting.

The cost of such a railway around 1900 is interesting, £900 per mile being the sum quoted. This estimate was made up as follows:—

Rails at 40 lb per yard, 63 tons at £5	–	£315	0	0
Fish Plates, 48 cwt at 7s	–	16	16	0
Bolts, 17 cwt at 16s	–	13	12	0
Sleepers, 2,200 at 1s 4d	–	147	0	0
Spikes, 40 cwt at 12s	–	24	0	0
Stobs, 3,520 at 4d	–	58	13	0
Fence wire and staples	–	12	0	0
Forming, 1,760 yards at 1s 6d	–	132	0	0
Ballasting 6 ft x 1 ft = 2/3 cubic yard per linear yard 1,173 cubic yards at 1s 6d	–	88	0	0
		807	1	0
Contingencies, say		92	19	0
		£900	0	0

The operating cost excluding the rent and wayleave which were agreed with the Duke, was quite low. Even in those days, Galloway complained that the amount required for upkeep, repairs, purchase of locomotives and wagons was constantly varying and usually rising. He then allowed £150 per annum for these items. To haul 22,000 tons for the 4.7 miles, his estimate was: —

Drivers' wages	–	£144
Surfacemen's wages	–	98
Coal for locos, 460 tons at 8s	–	184
Upkeep of rolling stock	–	150
Renewal of rails etc	–	50
Renewal of sleepers	–	56
		£682

This was equal to $7\frac{1}{2}$d per ton for the whole distance or slightly over $1\frac{1}{2}$d per ton per mile. Most of the traction took place during the winter months when coal was in demand and Galloway often moaned about his idle asset during the summer months. Had the railway been used all year the cost per ton could have been reduced further.

T. L. Galloway was obviously a disciple of Charles Spooner in advocating narrow gauge railways wherever possible. Indeed, he went further and advocated one common narrow gauge to be adopted in the United Kingdom as had been established in Belgium, France and other continental countries, for secondary lines.

CHAPTER FOUR

The Campbeltown & Machrihanish Light Railway

THE GENESIS OF THE RAILWAY

T. Lindsay Galloway, the colliery engineer, was always seeking ways of increasing the utilisation of his plant. Mention has already been made of his attempts to start glass and bottle making as a market for the good sandstone to be found just above the main coal. It rankled in his mind that he was forced to use the outmoded method of transporting coal-in-the-hutch on flat wagons and as early as 1902 he had been regretting that he could find no economic justification for purchasing bigger wagons. The transhipment of the coal from the coal ree to the ships by cart was limited to 150 tons per day and the existing railway wagons could handle this easily. Bigger wagons would merely mean fewer trains.

Because of the transhipment difficulty most of the colliery's output was consumed locally in Campbeltown and was therefore very seasonal. Traffic on the railway was lightest in the summer at the very time when improved weather and long daylight hours gave it increased capacity. But the railway only carried coal. Galloway must have looked enviously at the horse-drawn charabancs and wagonettes toiling over the road from one coast to another taking day-trippers and holiday-makers to Machrihanish as Salt Pans or Mary Pans as it had come to be called.

Local enterprise had not taken long to cash in on the new turbine steamer service. During the summers of 1901-3 135,000 people were carried by The Turbine Steamers Ltd to and from Campbeltown. Twenty-two thousand of these were booked through to Machrihanish. This was in addition to passengers carried by the Campbeltown Shipping Co's steamers.

Campbeltown Harbour, 1905. A horse brake hurries along the Old Quay to meet the approaching ss *Davaar*

To carry this number of people by horse-drawn traffic on earth-bound roads was no mean feat in itself.

It is not surprising that Galloway and other interested parties should get together to see if the colliery railway could be upgraded to something better. In the spring of 1904 the Association of Argyll Railway Co Ltd was formed with a capital of only £1,500.

T. L. Galloway did his homework well. Before anything had been done officially, he had surveyed the ground for extensions to the railway at both ends. On one occasion he was physically ejected from private land in Campbeltown and charged with trespass (against which there is no law in Scotland). When he put up a counter claim of assault the matter was dropped. The carriage and wagon builders were also asked to tender for rolling stock, passenger cars and coal wagons. The latter were designed with a view to the quick discharge of their contents into waiting ships, either by lifting bodily or by having detachable pallets which the crane would empty into waiting vessels.

As far as his dealings with the Duke of Argyll were concerned T. L. Galloway wasn't so successful. His Grace was directly involved as the ground through which any extensions would be made belonged eventually to him and naturally he wanted to be paid for it. What is more he wanted more than its agricultural value. The application for a light railway was opposed by His Grace and arguments of the pros and cons of the situation were thrashed out in legal circles for years. It was not until January 1909 that John Douglas Sutherland Campbell received his settlement: £1,722 13s 4d.

An application for a light railway order was made in April 1904 and the Light Railway Commissioners held a public inquiry in Campbeltown on 28 September that year. As well as the Duke's opposition, many of his tenants also opposed the application as they felt the railway would reduce the value of the land through which it passed. The Light Railway order was passed by the Commissioners in February 1905 after some amendments and the railway was finally incorporated under the Light Railways Act of 8 May.

Various other meetings were held during the summer of 1904 when the proposals to extend the line were put both privately and publicly to the people of the district. The general feeling in Campbeltown was favourable but dissenting voices were heard. The narrow gauge of 2 ft 3 in was thought by these, uninformed of the successes of even narrower rails elsewhere, to be impossible for passenger carrying. There were remarks that the engines, the existing ones, 'didn't look much like passenger engines'. This was probably quite true but to each attack there was a satisfactory answer. The Campbeltown town council was alarmed at the prospect of a level crossing over Kilkerran Road but strangely enough less perturbed about the terminus in Hall Street.

A feature of the opposition to the railway in its early days was the issue by a local bookseller of a series of 'funny' post-cards. These showed various disorganised happenings in cartoon form on a railway purporting to be the c & m l r but bearing no pictorial likeness. The humour was very heavy and a typical card showed a conductor collecting fares inside a longitudinal-seated car, the caption being:

Campbeltown & Machrihanish Light Railway
First car through rural district
Tram Conductor (rustic) 'Here, ladies and gentlemen there's something wrong with my "Fare Bill", you'll ALL have to pay again'.

Different forms of traction were considered and in addition to steam, electric and petrol-driven cars were considered. The last two would certainly have pushed the railway completely into the tramway class, especially as overhead current collection was proposed. It would have been extremely difficult to arrange for conventional nose hung tramway motors of the period to be fitted between 2 ft 3 in gauge wheels and this may well have been the deciding factor. Otherwise the c & m would have been a sister to the Rothesay and Etrick Bay Tramway or the Manx Electric Railway! At this time the question of widening the gauge was being considered, and when the new locomotives were ordered, there was a proviso that they be arranged for the possible conversion later to 2 ft 6 in gauge. However, by the spring of 1905 most of the difficulties had been resolved and the new company got down to business in earnest.

THE PROSPECTUS

The company's prospectus was issued by the lawyers Messrs Wright, Johnson & Mackenzie of Glasgow on 5 June 1905. The prospectus announced that the company would acquire from the Campbeltown Coal Company Ltd, the existing mineral railway from the coal company's colliery near Machrihanish to the coal depot at Campbeltown. It would extend that railway to the harbour at Campbeltown and to the golf links at Machrihanish. The light railway as authorised was intended for passenger and goods traffic between Campbeltown and Machrihanish and for the carriage of coal and other minerals between the colliery and Campbeltown town and the harbour.

Machrihanish, with its attractive golf links was considered a rapidly-rising seaside resort and the opening of the railway should greatly develop it from a residential standpoint. The railway would also be favourably placed in securing the custom of the steamer passengers previously mentioned. It was hoped that, in addition to the tourist and golfing traffic, a considerable amount of local passenger, general goods and farm produce traffic would develop, as Campbeltown had a population of over 8,000 and the railway ran through the finest agricultural part of Kintyre.

An agreement was made with the Campbeltown Coal Company by which the coal company was bound to send all its traffic from the colliery over the railway at a fixed rate. Seventy thousand tons per annum of coal and other minerals was anticipated, most of which would be for shipment. 'The coal should be sufficient to last for generations.' There were also several seams of fireclay which it was hoped could be exploited for brickmaking.

The Campbeltown Coal Company agreed to sell the existing mineral railway as it stood with the locomotives etc for the sum of £4,500 and to subscribe for 6,500 shares in the railway company.

The total capital outlay required for constructing and working the railway was estimated as follows:—

Permanent Way	£13,237
Rolling Stock	2,576
Signalling Apparatus	900
Land, Cost of Obtaining Order	
Working Capital	6,287
	£23,000

The revenue to be derived from the railway was estimated:—

Traffic	
Passenger	£1,300
Minerals	1,250
General Goods etc	300
	£2,850
Estimate of working cuts	1,531
Profit	£1,319

This on a capital outlay of £23,000 represented 5 per cent with a margin for contingencies or additional dividend. The capital which the company was authorised to raise was £26,000 and initially £23,000 was issued in shares of £1 each. Of that amount £13,050 had already been applied for and subscriptions were sought for the remaining £9,950. A form of application was included in the make-up of the prospectus. The company was empowered to issue debenture stock for £2,000.

It was hoped that the railway would be open for passenger traffic before the end of 1905 but in the meantime mineral traffic would continue to be carried by the railway company over the existing line. Thus the company would begin to earn revenue at once.

The directors named on the prospectus were:—

Col John M. Denny MP, of Messrs Wm. Denny & Bros
Shipbuilders, Dumbarton
James Fergusson, distiller, Glasgow
James J. Galloway, engineer, Glasgow
James Wood, coalmaster, Glasgow

T. Lindsay Galloway was named as the company's engineer.

The light railway order was typical of many passed about that time and concerns itself chiefly with the protection of the legal rights of the general public who should not be inconvenienced by the building or working of the new railway.

The Argyll Railway Company Ltd and all other persons who subscribed were henceforth known as the Campbeltown & Machrihanish Light Railway Company and as such was a composite body. The normal company requirements of a registered office (in Glasgow), and regular meetings etc were outlined and the number of directors fixed at between three and seven.

The railways authorised were : —

> Railway No 1 : 4 furlongs 6 chains from the Christian Institute in Hall Street, along the foreshore and thence to join the existing mineral railway some 14 chains from its eastern terminus.
> Railway No 2 : 1 furlong of sidings on the New Quay.
> Railway No 3 : 4 miles 5 furlongs 7½ chains, namely the existing mineral railway.
> Railway No 4 : 7 furlongs 6 chains from a juncture 1 furlong 7 chains from the western terminus of the mineral railway to the back of the Ugadale Arms Hotel at Machrihanish.

The act specified a rail gauge of 2 ft 3 in or any other which the Board of Trade may approve and also stated that the motive power should be steam, electricity or some other. The company was empowered to erect overhead conductor wire carried on posts and all the other equipment necessary for electric traction. The authority was given for the compulsory purchase of land provided it was taken within three years. This compulsory purchase forbad the acquisition of ten or more houses belonging to the 'labouring classes' and defined these as persons having an income of less than 30s per week. The railway was to be completed within five years.

The company was required to provide gates or some form of cattle guard at all local crossings. If gates were provided, an official crossing keeper was to be employed and the gates kept closed to the railway except when trains were passing. Where ungated crossings existed, speed restriction boards specifying the maximum speed to drivers were required at 300 yards on either side of the crossing and warning notices on the road at fifty yards each side. The company was responsible for the maintenance of the road surface for 7 ft on either side of any level crossing. At the Kilkerran Road crossing, the railway was required to remove the high stone wall on the south side of the road to enable engine drivers to see their way clear across the road. A new wall or screen of trees was to be provided to preserve the privacy of the adjoining private property belonging to Captain Stewart. The company was expressly forbidden from adjusting the height of the public road at Kilkerran crossing although elsewhere this was allowed within limits. Trains were not permitted to stand on level crossings.

On the north side of the Kilkerran crossing, the order insisted that the ground between the existing foreshore and the new railway embankment be filled in. All sewage and drainage pipes involved were to be extended or deviated at the railway's expense.

Should the railway for any reason cease to carry passengers for more than six months, the farmer landowners would have the right to repossess their lands on payment of the purchase price.

The railway would not be allowed to open without Board of Trade approval and severe penalties were involved if this was contravened. Similar penalties would be imposed if traffic commenced without the inspector's requirements being fulfilled.

The order specified that no vehicle might have an axle load greater than 8 tons on the railway unless relaid with rail of greater than 50 lb per yard when the axle load could be 10 tons. The maximum speed on open track was fixed at 20 mph; 15 mph on gradients steeper than 1 in 50; 10 mph on curves sharper than $4\frac{1}{2}$ chains; and 5 mph on all ungated level crossings. The Board of Trade reserved the right to impose any other speed limits as it thought fit.

If other than steam traction were adopted, specific permission for alternative forms of mechanical propulsion had to be obtained. Should electric traction be envisaged, all kinds of safeguards were imposed to prevent damage of such items as gas and water pipes, and telephone lines from corrosion by electrolytic action, induced currents etc.

When the railway ran along Hall Street, it was deemed a street tramway and became subject to the many features of restrictive legislation imposed on such undertakings. The railway was required to maintain the road surface between its rails and to 18 in either side of them. Normal road traffic could still use and wear this surface which the railway had to pay for and did not use itself. No more than 100 yards of paving might be opened up at any one time and the maximum time allowed for any repairs on such an opening was four weeks. It was the railway's job to provide barriers, lights at night, and a watchman when the road surface was so disturbed. If this was not enough, any road material removed from a repair site and replaced by new remained the property of the local authority who had the power to insist on its transport to any place of its choice within a mile of the scene. The only advantage the railway seemed to have was that the general public were not allowed to use vehicles fitted with flanged wheels on the railway maintained piece of roadway, in other words on the rails themselves, and were liable for a £20 fine for doing so. The rails on the New Quay and Hall Street were to be flush with the road surface to permit the free passage of ordinary road vehicles. Although the C & M L R order does not specifically mention the fact, the rails in Hall Street which were deemed passenger-carrying lines were of the street tramway flanged type.

Should the railway at any time abandon the street portion, it would restore the roadway to its original condition at its own expense.

The Campbeltown authorities were given the right to make by-laws governing the stopping of trains, condition of loading, and the hours of traffic for the street tramway part of the line.

The maximum charge for 1st class passengers (of whom there were none anyway) was fixed at 3d per mile, and for 3rd class passengers 1d per mile, less than three miles counting as three miles. Rates for excursion traffic were not so fixed and the company could charge what they liked on special trains.

First class passengers were to be allowed 120 lb of luggage free and 3rd class passengers 60 lb. Rates for the carriage of other types of goods were specified in detail in a separate schedule. A second schedule attached to the order specified various requirements for the permanent way. The rail was to weigh not less than 40 lb per yard. All curves of less than 3 chains were to be checkrailed. The rails at the joints and sharp curves were to be secured to the sleepers by fang bolts or double spiking with bearing plates. On sharp curves the gauge was to be maintained by steel ties.

No turntables were required by statute but no tender engine was to be allowed to run tender first at more than 15 mph.

At the discretion of the Board of Trade, electrical communication might or might not be required but their ruling would be enforced.

Where passing loops were provided, there was to be a home signal at or near the entry points for each direction of running. A distant signal must also be provided if the home signal was not visible from a quarter mile away. The signals were required to fly to and remain at danger if any failure in the operating mechanism took place. The signals were to be interlocked with the points and with each other.

Either platforms, or a convenient means of access from the ground to the passenger cars were stipulated. The company was under no obligation to provide shelter or conveniences at any station or stopping place.

The Campbeltown & Machrihanish Light Railway Order was finally confirmed by the Board of Trade on 30 May 1908.

CONSTRUCTION

The contract for the building of the extension was granted to Messrs James Young & Co in November 1905. Work began almost immediately. The Machrihanish extension required little in the way of earthworks but the new eastern line was another matter. The new roadbed had to descend rapidly from the junction at the Limecraigs rifle range to the Kilkerran Road through a cutting, not deep by normal standards, but deeper than anything hitherto encountered by Galloway's railway. The digging was done by pick and shovel in the time-honoured manner. The first cut was steep sided to allow a line of rails to be laid and on these the contractor used his own wooden dump trucks pulled by horses. The spoil from the cutting was carried across the Kilkerran Road and couped (tipped) to form the embankment on the foreshore as far as the New Quay where the existing ground level was again met. The driving of the cutting was not without incident. On 14 April one of the workmen was severely injured on the work and on 2 June, Captain Duncan Stewart, still a rabid opponent of the railway, again assaulted T. L. Galloway and this time, Galloway, having his light railway order, took him to court where Captain Stewart was tried for his indiscretion on 10 August 1907.

The first big engine, *Argyll*, was delivered early in 1906 and taken by road on a wagon drawn by a traction engine to Plantation Crossing where it was set on the rails and probably started work immediately. The first carriage was delivered at the beginning of June and similarly transported, this time on two wagons. However, by the time the second carriage arrived a fortnight later, the railway had reached the harbour and the vehicle was set directly on to the rails. The other two carriages followed at fortnightly intervals.

The laying of the flanged rail in Hall Street led to an amusing little incident. Apparently the track-laying gang were gauging the rails, not by the inside of the rail head as is normally done, but by measuring the distance between the base flange, ie directly on the sleeper. This did not matter very much until the transition from normal flat-bottom rail to tramway type rail took place. The flanged rail section has an offset head so the gauge came out nearer 2 ft 5 in by this method of track laying. It was not until someone tried to run the construction train over the new track that the fault was discovered and the whole lot had to be relaid.

The flanged rail was only used on the straight track down Hall Street. The loop line was designated a siding and not con- sidered to be passenger carrying and was therefore laid in ordinary flat-bottomed rail. The difficulty of bending the flanged rail probably influenced this decision although some passenger trains started from the loop.

Meanwhile the existing colliery line was brought up to

Page 55 (above) *Storming up the bank past the rifle range;* (below) *Hungry Hoose crossing shortly after the Company was formed. Note the old alignment and the abandoned sharp curve which precluded the use of 6-coupled engines until 1906*

Page 56 (above) Passenger's eye view of Atlantic, *1930*. *Note the balcony railings and tip-over seats;* (below) *three fashionable young ladies alight at Machrihanish during the first summer of passenger operation*

Page 57 (above) *Machrihanish in 1906. Argyll and a 4-coach train are posed at Machrihanish for photography and for the frontispiece painting*; (below) *a single coach train at the Machrihanish buffer stops just before the end*

Page 58 (above) *Coach No 6 at Machrihanish showing door arrangement;* (below) *Machrihanish Station. The building housed the telegraph and block instruments and incorporated a buffet, shown on right. The fishbox is the one referred to in the text*

proper railway standards. The principle alteration was the provision of a passing loop and signals at Lintmill. The railway was realigned at Plantation Crossing to remove T. L. Galloway's thorn in the side in the form of the sharp curve. The steep gradient he was stuck with, but he hoped the bigger engines would do much to mitigate this problem.

The construction of the railway necessitated much Sunday work, which aroused the wrath of local Sabbatarians. As late as January 1907 the United Free Presbytery of Kintyre was condemning this action as against God's teachings and prophesying doom and ruination to the railway. Maybe that's where all the later trouble emanated from!

On 4 August an experimental trip over the new line was made and various employees at the colliery and others were invited. This was a fortuitous idea as the locomotive became derailed at various places and the miners alighted and lifted the engine back on to the rails.

INSPECTION AND OPENING

By 21 July the railway was about complete and some trial runs had been made. The final inspection by the Board of Trade officer Lt Col E. Druitt took place on 17 August.

The colonel was met at the steamer, *Queen Alexandra*, by T. Lindsay Galloway and taken over the new railway. They were accompanied by various people associated with Campbeltown and the Clyde, including Captain John Williamson and Mr Wishart, who were directors of the railway company; Mr Wm. Johnston the company's solicitor; Mr Drummond and Mr Gilchrist representing the contractor; and Mr J. Gibson of Messrs Tyer & Co. The party also included the Provost and Master of Works of Campbeltown, the manager of Argyll Colliery, and Alexander Black, the new Superintendent of the railway, late of the Caledonian Railway.

Col Druitt rode on the step of the carriage and examined the permanent way as the train proceeded with the engine propelling the coach. It stopped for the examination of each junction in turn to test the levers and locking gear. The steel girder bridge over the Chiscan Water was tested by the simple expedient of running the train over it at full speed while

D

Col Druitt observed it from the ground. The signals, levers and points etc at Lintmill were given a searching examination. The train then proceeded to Machrihanish. The return trip was made at full speed all the way to test the riding of the train which was apparently excellent and the good colonel was able to catch the return sailing of the *Queen Alexandra* without trouble. His report is as follows:—

> Railway Department,
> Board of Trade,
> 8 Richmond Terrace,
> Whitehall,
> London. S.W.
> *21 Aug 06*

Sir,

I have the honour to report for the information of the Board of Trade that in compliance with the instructions contained in your minute of 8th August I have inspected the light railways authorised by the Campbeltown & Machrihanish Light Railway Order of 1905. The railways inspected for passenger traffic are No 1, No 3 /part of/ and No 4 forming a continuous line 5 miles 71.2 chains in length.

The gauge is 2 ft 3 ins and the line is single throughout with the exception of a passing place at Lintmill.

The steepest gradient is 1 in 35 and the sharpest curve has a radius of 5.4 chains.

The deepest cutting has a depth of 28 ft and the highest embankment a height of 6 ft.

Width at formation level is 10 ft.

The rails are flat bottomed and mostly weigh 50 lbs per yard but some short length of the line have rails of 40 lbs per yard. The sleepers are of Baltic red wood creosoted 4 ft-6 ft long x 9 ins x 4 ins and there are 12 sleepers per 30 ft rail.

The rails are attached to the sleepers by fang bolts at the ends and by spikes at the intermediate points and are connected by fishplates. The ballast is of ashes or broken stone.

The fencing is of varying height mostly 3 ft 6 ins.

There is only one underbridge on the line span 20 ft formed by 4 rolled steel joists with cross timbers resting on all 4 joists which are connected by cross beams. The abutments are of concrete.

There are 3 culverts 2 formed of timber beams of 7 ft and 6 ft respectively and 1 of concrete.

The steelworks of the bridge gave moderate deflection under test load and have sufficient theoretical strength.

There are no viaducts, tunnels or stations on the line.

There are 3 public road level crossings; no gates are provided but there are cattle guards and the usual notices on each side in the roadway and speed boards 5 miles an hour erected as required by Section 28 of the Order.

There are 7 private road level crossings including the road to the rifle range with no gates and at these there are no cattle guards.

All these private road crossings should be provided with cattle guards to prevent animals straying on to the line.

There are the following ground frames:

1. At the junctions of the siding to the New Quay at Campbeltown.

2. At the junction of the colliery sidings between Campbeltown and Lintmill.

3. At the junction of the colliery sidings near Machrihanish. These are all 2 lever frames controlled by the train staff/tablet/ for the section of the line Nos 1 & 2 Campbeltown to Lintmill and No 3 Lintmill to Machrihanish.

There is a similar ground frame at Machrihanish terminus for controlling the outlet points of the run round.

At Lintmill passing place is a raised ground frame for working the points and signals containing 8 working and 2 spare levers. The interlocking and other arrangements at these frames is satisfactory. No lock bars are provided for the facing points of the passing loop and care must be taken not to move the points until the tail of the train has passed over them.

I attach an undertaking as to the mode of working the line viz 1 engine in steam or 2 coupled together to be allowed in each of the sections at one time.

Such engine to carry the staff/tablet for the section. As it is anticipated that the line will be equipped with the Electric Tablet system in course of time a tablet is to be used in lieu of a train staff for the present. This mode of working may be approved. I also attach the order to firing on the rifle range across the railway when trains are passing.

The old part of the line viz Railway No 3 is in pretty good order but on the new railway No 1 the ballasting is not completed and this should be gone on with as quickly as possible. This Railway is on a steep gradient of 1 in 40 down to the level crossing of the Kilkerran Road and speed down the incline to the Quay should be limited to 5 miles an hour.

The rodding and locking apparatus at the points on the quay at Campbeltown require boxing in.

Buffer stops are required at the terminus of the line at Machrihanish.

The rolling stock is fitted with a Norwegian hook centre buffer coupling, the hooks being secured by chains passed round them which should always be secured.

The carriages are 43 ft 6 ins over headstocks with bogies 30 ft centre to centre. These are I think too long for use on the sharper curves and any future stock should be shorter. The trains are to be fitted throughout with the Vacuum Automatic Brake.

For the present maximum speed on the line should not exceed 15 miles an hour. This restriction may be removed at the discretion of the engineer when the ballasting is complete.

The fencing in places on the old No 3 line needs repair.

Subject to the above remarks . . . I can recommend the Board of Trade to sanction the use of the above Railways for Passenger Traffic.

> I have etc,
> /Sd./ E. Druitt,
> Lt Col R. E.

The railway was authorised to be opened forthwith and the first run with fare paying passengers took place on the following day, 18 August 1906, when several of the steamer passengers travelled on the train.

The official opening was on 25 August and within three weeks 10,000 passengers had availed themselves of the service.

CHAPTER FIVE

The Wee Train

THE ROUTE DESCRIBED

Unlike most railways, even quite minor ones, the town terminus of the Campbeltown & Machrihanish was not on private ground. The locomotive and carriage depot was nearly a mile away. Thus the first introduction to the 'wee train' for most people was their finding one of the 0–6–2 tanks and its train of carriages standing in the street at the head of the Old Quay. At Towyn or Portmadoc in Wales, Douglas in the Isle of Man, even at Central Station in Glasgow, only the potential passenger saw the trains at close quarters. In Campbeltown, the train was right there amongst the throng and everyone, visitor and local inhabitant alike was familiar with it whether they were travelling on it or not. This appears to be a sure way of finding a place in everyone's heart. This same impact was to be seen where various tramway undertakings once operated and the trams became local pets.

To describe the c & m's Campbeltown terminus therefore is to describe the harbour and Hall Street. The harbour was roughly in the form of a square formed by two piers, the Old Quay and the New Quay. The latter despite its name was over 100 years old and the Old Quay even more so. The two piers were L-shaped to make the harbour almost completely enclosed, the narrow entrance being between their extremities. In the corner formed between the head of the New Quay and Hall Street there was, and still is, a broad slipway to enable fishing boats to be drawn up for fitting out. The Old Quay was built of stone as far as the end but the front of the pier was substantially built on timber piling. The upper surface on the timber frame was paved with granite sets and the pier build-

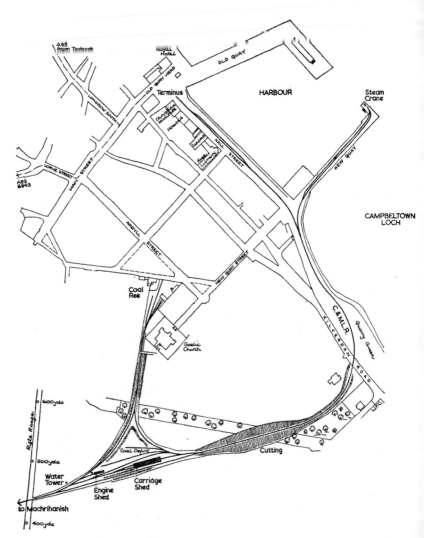

LAYOUT AT CAMPBELTOWN 1906 TO 1934

ings were built of brick. The Old Quay was similarly of stone with a timber front. The interior of the harbour partly dried out at low tide but sailing coasters and 'puffers' could moor on the Hall Street side of the pier. This resulted in several pictures of the railway engines apparently carrying masts and spars or even square rigged topsails! The Old Quay was invariably used as the passenger steamer pier and also for general merchandise for which there was a hand-operated crane on its north-west side. The New Quay was more of the nature of a breakwater and only its front face and harbour side were arranged for use. Apart from wartime occupation by the Royal Navy, the only serious use of the New Quay for handling freight was when the railway used it for shipping coal.

Campbeltown Main Street runs from the Old Quay head through the oldest part of the town to Castlehill Church. Where it joints the Old Quay and Hall Street, a small square has been formed. When the railway arrived this square was bounded on the town side by the offices of the Campbeltown Steamship Company, the Christian Institute and a vacant site on which, shortly after the railway's arrival, was built the Royal Hotel. Within the square stand a weigh bridge and weigh house and in recent times they have been joined by an ancient Celtic Cross which formerly stood in the High Street. This cross now forms the centrepiece of a traffic roundabout.

The Christian Institute was side on to the railway and adjoining it was Royal Avenue, a block of tenement houses which nowadays would be called flats. The ground floor of these was given over to shops and the last shop was the 'Railway Office'. It served as booking office, signal box, parcels office and everything else one normally finds at a railway terminus. Proceeding along Hall Street, the remaining buildings in railway days were the 'Argyll Photographic Studio' which was a small wooden building, a cinema, and the Campbeltown Free Library which is also the town's museum. After this there were no buildings immediately on Hall Street until the New Quay head where there was a stone shed used by the RNLI and here road traffic had to turn right up New Quay Street.

The railway tracks ended level with the corner of the Christian Institute and the coaches were propelled right to the end to be as near the steamer traffic as possible. In fact nearer than possible if the grooves cut in the road surface beyond the rail ends were anything to go by! About a coach length from the rail ends the run-round loop points turned off on the harbour side of the straight line. As previously mentioned the straight track was laid in flanged tramway rail while the loop and points were of ordinary flat bottomed rail. The loop was long enough for the engine to run round the original four carriages but when longer trains were run, the marshalling became complicated.

The most common type of photograph of the C & M L R shows a passenger train standing in the Hall Street terminus with the Christian Institute prominent in the background. A study of these photographs shows that in early days the tower of the Christian Institute had four large stone balls round its base at roof level but on later pictures after 1925 one of these balls is missing! One wonders who was below when it came down.

Once past the loop the single line ran along the centre of Hall Street until New Quay head was reached and the line assumed the independence normally associated with railways.

The track on the New Quay was double for its entire length with a trailing crossover half way along. At the outer end of the quay the tracks turned sharply left and converged on a cradle which could be lifted by the adjacent steam crane. This vertical boilered steam crane was rail mounted on a short length of standard gauge (4 ft 8½ in) track, the ends of which were turned up like ski points. As well as its normal functions, this crane was used as makeshift diving board by local youth. In addition to the crane there was a capstan at the end of the pier which was used to pull single wagons on to the cradle for loading into waiting vessels. Loaded coal trains would be positioned on one road of the pier and the other kept free for empties. When a ship was loading coal, each loaded wagon would be hand shunted by capstan on to the cradle which would then be lifted by the crane and swung out over the ship. Before lifting, the wagon end door pins would be freed so that it only needed a pull on a rope to tilt the entire cradle and the wagon's contents were discharged into the hold of the ship. The cradle was then returned and the wagon run off down the empties road for collection later. This method of loading coal was very common in the Ayrshire ports until comparatively recently but with the decline in Scottish coal mining it can only now be seen in use occasionally. It is quite amazing how smoothly even twelve ton standard gauge coal wagons can be handled by this method.

On coming off the New Quay, the two tracks converged and curved round to meet the main line on the reclaimed ground. The points at the junction here were controlled with a ground frame interlocked with the tablet and normally set to the Hall Street direction. From here the railway ran along the foreshore on the new formation which was also open to the public on foot. Budding athletes were wont to race the train here; not too difficult a feat as the train had to slow down to 5 mph before swinging right over the Kilkerran Road. Once over the crossing, the engines would be opened up to tackle the 1 in 35 gradient and the typical Barclay exhaust of the big engines would echo all round the bay as they pounded up the cutting. The cutting was allegedly private but the local populace soon found it a convenient short cut and very soon it was being used as a public footpath—the purpose which it officially serves today.

At the top end of the cutting was situated Limecraigs depot where the railway company had its workshops. While the main line thundered on up the hill on a low embankment, the carriage sheds and sidings were down on the right at ground level. They were encompassed by the other two sides of a triangle also on low embankments as was the single-road engine shed. As a result, the gradient out of the carriage shed was very steep indeed. One of the sidings behind the carriage shed was in the form of a loop. The carriage shed had two roads each capable of storing two carriages. It was of wooden construction with a curved corrugated iron roof. On its main line side and cut into the embankment was the sand drier with its associated chimney and a locker for the carbide gas equipment. On one occasion the manager, Alexander Black, was poking around in the carbide locker with a lighted match and blew his eyebrows off.

The engine shed was also of wood with a gable roof sporting a row of five smoke vents and could take two engines. Outside

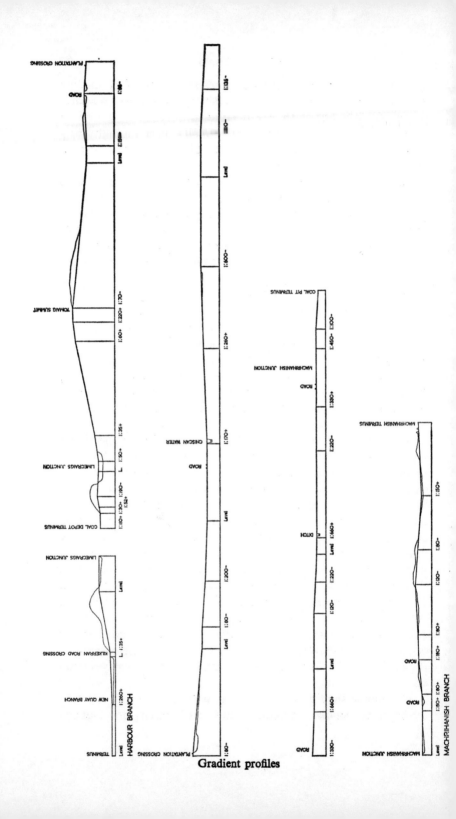

Gradient profiles

the engine shed was a platform used for coaling the engines. Both the engine shed and the carriage shed were entered from the old mineral line while the two coal sidings faced the harbour and were connected to the new curve between the old coal ree and the cutting. In the apex of the triangle a vegetable plot was worked by the railway manager.

The original mineral line to the coal ree was doubled between the engine shed and a point about half way down the old stone cutting. By the time the C & M L R was using this line, the Kintyre Nurseries, which were situated on either side of the cutting, were using an overbridge to connect their grounds. This was the Railway's only overbridge and was made from two I girders with a wooden deck and railings. The layout at the coal ree had previously featured a side-loading platform where the hutches could be run off sideways and later emptied. The layout was now modified to form a five-road fan, three of which were very short and ended against a platform to facilitate the hand-emptying of the end-door wagons of coal for domestic distribution. Some of the coal was sold in iron two-wheeled barrows which the customer took away, unloaded and then brought back empty.

Just before the old mineral line met the new harbour line, the engines' water column was placed. This was a rather mean thing consisting of a bent goose-neck pipe with a piece of hose attached, the whole supported by a shaky wooden tripod. At both ends of the triangle the points were interlocked with the tablet and were normally set to the new main line.

The entire site of the triangle is now occupied by a football pitch which gives an idea of how much was packed into the space.

Immediately uphill from the depot the rifle range crossed the railway at right angles. The 500 yd and 600 yd firing butts were on the right, on the flat, while the rest of the range rose steeply on the left up the Barley Bannocks Hill, one of the foothills of Beinn Ghuilean. Special regulations were enforced about the respective rights of way of the train and the bullets to ensure that the two should not coincide. A red flag was flown when firing was in progress and the train was expected to stop and wait. While the possibility of spinning yarns is enormous, the train does not appear to actually have been

shot up and the story of passengers having to flatten themselves on the floor can never be exploited.

The main line climbed remorselessly up the hill to Tomaig,
now on the old colliery line formation, and clearly fenced
with wooden posts and wire on both sides. The strain posts on
this fence were steel with diagonal bracing and many of these
were so firmly planted that they have long outlived their
wooden compatriots. At Plantation Crossing where the railway had been realigned, the old track remained for some time
after the opening. It was necessary to reinstate the gates at this
crossing and again the crossing keeper was a woman, Annie
Macdonald (later Mrs Colville). This lady eventually purchased
the crossing keeper's house from the railway when the line
closed down.

Immediately over the Aros Road crossing was situated the
Lintmill passing loop. The signals here, two homes and two
starters, were carried on lattice posts and the arms were lower
quadrant of the same type as those used on main line railways.
Red and green spectacle glasses were provided but the signals
never appear to have been lit at night. The lever frame was
housed in a small wooden signal box having a flat roof. The
floor was raised about 3 ft above ground level and there were
steps and a small balcony on the Machrihanish end of the
building. Although there were windows at each end and along
the front, those at the front were always covered by a large
shutter hinged at the bottom and fitted with a hasp and padlock
at the top. The block instruments were housed here but the
box was seldom manned, the conductor on the train opening
it as required and operating the tablet release mechanism.

There was an official halt at the nearest point the line passed
Drumlemble village and the railway built a small shelter for
waiting passengers. Unfortunately the shelter was shamefully
abused and was seldom in a fit state for its normal use.

The new line to Machrihanish branched off to the left at
West Machrihanish Farm and the original line ran straight on
to the colliery. The junction points here were also locked by
the tablet. In the colliery, more tracks were provided and the
layout altered to be more suitable for the new wagons which
could be loaded directly from above. The older type had had
the hutches run on to them sideways from the winding cage.

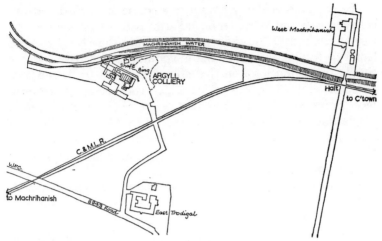

LAYOUT AT ARGYLL COLLIERY

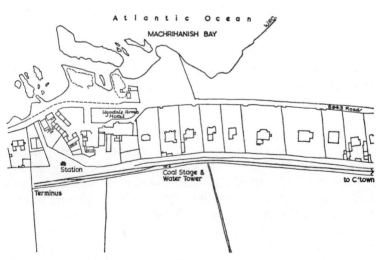

LAYOUT AT MACHRIHANISH

0   1/4 Mile

The new line to Machrihanish crossed the main road midway between East and West Trodigal Farms and swung due west to run along behind the then new villas and the Ugadale Arms Hotel to terminate behind the mission hall. Here there was a simple run-round loop on the left of the main track and at a later period a siding was added which converted the westernmost point to a facing crossover. As in Hall Street, the loop would not take all six carriages and when a long train arrived some fancy fly shunting had to be resorted to with carriages being controlled on the handbrake by the guard or in later days by the conductress.

The area on the north side of the tracks was surfaced with red blaze from the colliery's bing. The station building here was a neat wooden chalet with a corrugated iron roof which overhung both sides. It fulfilled the same function as the railway office shop at the opposite end of the line and housed the block and tablet instruments. In addition there was a kiosk built on to the eastern side of the building which purveyed cigarettes etc to the passengers. Generally speaking, only passenger trains came into the terminus but occasionally the siding was used for storing stock and the big brake van spent most of its life there as an additional storehouse.

At the Campbeltown end of the station area there was a staging for coaling engines and a standpipe for water.

The railway had a two-wire telephone line carried on poles throughout its length.

OF SAFETY REGULATIONS

During the second half of the nineteenth century, it had become obvious that if passenger trains were going to run regularly at high speeds, something more than the locomotive's brakes augmented by a brake van would be required. Two main braking systems were evolved, the air brake and the vacuum brake, and on each system power was taken from the locomotive to each carriage for the purpose of operating brakes thereon. By the turn of the century all the big railway companies had adopted one or other of the systems.

On light railways, automatic brakes are not obligatory and to this day some manage without them. However, the Camp-

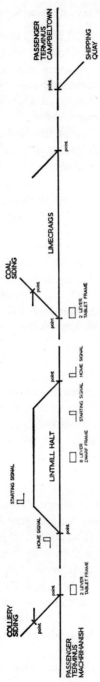

Signalling diagram

beltown & Machrihanish Light Railway decided that its passenger trains would be vacuum braked. Each carriage had two vacuum cylinders operating the brakes on the adjacent bogie. When the vacuum was created by the engine's ejector, it applied equally to both sides of a double acting cylinder. As the cylinders were mounted vertically, the piston lay at the bottom by its own weight and the brakes were off. When the driver destroyed the vacuum, he was only able to do so on the lower side of the piston and atmospheric pressure immediately operated to push the piston upwards and apply the brakes. A broken train pipe or the train dividing had the same effect. Two side chains were also provided on each buffer beam to act as an additional safeguard but these were seldom used. In fact one of the fitters confessed in later years to not knowing what they were for! Side chains had been a feature of main line stock before automatic brakes became universal but by 1906 they were obsolete. To release the brakes, the locomotive had to regenerate the vacuum each time using the larger of its two ejectors. To prevent the brakes 'leaking on' and dragging should all the seals not be perfect, a second small ejector was kept on continuously when the train was running and even this consumed a fair amount of the boiler's steam.

The two big engines were themselves fitted with vacuum brakes although single acting cylinders were employed as the 'fail safe' aspect was not required. The tiny *Princess* was also fitted with vacuum hoses at each end and ejectors but did not herself have vacuum brake cylinders. If the carriages stopped so did *Princess*. Otherwise her original handbrake would suffice.

In respect of signalling, light railways enjoyed a degree of freedom from legislation provided speeds were limited. Generally on such lines the rule 'one engine in steam' was enough to cover all eventualities. The C & M L R had too much traffic to be thus restricted and adopted a system modified from main line practice. The equipment was supplied by Messrs Tyer & Co Ltd and was similar to that adopted by the New Zealand Railways. It was almost unique in its facility for allowing the crews to operate it rather than requiring a signalman who would have to remain at his post until the train had cleared the section.

Until very recently, British practice on single line working

Page 75 (above) *Stephen McCabe, Superintendent's son, in front of train at Machrihanish;* (below) Atlantic *'on shed' with her crew, Stewart McQuaig and Jimmy McGougan*

Page 76 (above) *Coach body at Trench Point 1954;* (below) Atlantic *on demolition train at Limecraigs, June 1934*

Page 77 *The colliery engines in* C & M L R *days.* (above) Chevalier *as rebuilt with a home made cab and* Princess's *sandbox 12.5.25;* (below) *the remains of* Princess *on the same day*

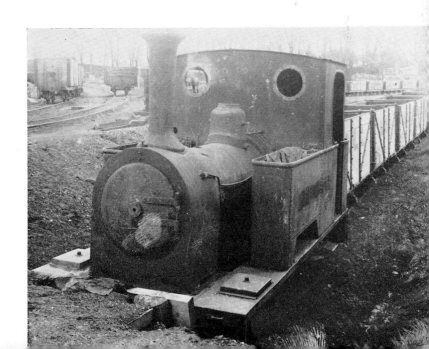

Page 78 Limecraigs shed. Left to right water column, o–6–2T and small wagons, large wagons on lower track centre, coaling stage, engine shed, small wagons, carriages, carriage shed and main line

has been to divide the railway into sections. For each section one token is available and the engine driver must be in possession of it before he has authority to enter the next single line section. Should two trains be travelling in the same direction one behind the other, the token would have to be sent back by a man on a horse or bicycle, as indeed happened in some places. However the system was enlarged to allow several identical tokens to exist, each of which could be fitted into an electric telegraph instrument such that when one key was removed from any such instrument, all the other keys, or tablets as they are known, became locked in. Thus a driver on clearing a section hands over the tablet and when it is placed in the instrument there, a second tablet is available at the preceding station to allow the following train to come on. The tablet is also arranged to act as a key to unlock any pointwork on the main line, and in doing so the tablet is locked in the point lever mechanism until the points are reset at normal. The system would appear to be foolproof but its originators had reckoned without the men of Kintyre. As early as the February after the opening of the line, one of the point mechanisms in Hall Street had been tampered with to the extent that a carriage was derailed there. In February the following year, the railway had other trouble from vandalism and two youths were arrested and charged with stealing metal piping from the railway.

Prior to the summer of 1910 the last train of the day was the 5.10 pm from Machrihanish to Campbeltown and the same engine and crew started work the following morning at 5.40 am. Now the depot at Limecraigs lay in the middle of the Lintmill—Campbeltown tablet section and the tablet was required to open the depot points. The train would arrive in Hall Street and, after unloading its passengers, the empty carriages were taken up the cutting to the carriage sheds. The points were unlocked and the carriages put to bed for the night. The engine was coaled and watered and left in the shed with the tablet stored comfortably away in the cab. As this engine was first out next day this practice was quite inoffensive.

However, during the summer of 1910, Alexander Black, the superintendent, scheduled another train from Machrihanish to Campbeltown at 6.30 pm. This didn't suit Hugh Harper who

E

was the driver on the 5.10 pm one little bit. He was now required after tucking his engine up for the night, to reset the depot points, retrieve the tablet and set off down the cutting on foot to Hall Street and insert the tablet in the telegraph instrument in the railway office. By doing so, he could set the instrument at Lintmill to 'line clear' and the 6.10 pm train driver could withdraw his tablet and proceed. This could involve Harper in all of half an hour each evening but what was worse, a similar half hour was needed each following morning to reverse the proceedings.

Hugh Harper had been on the Caledonian Railway for four years before coming to the C & M in 1909 and the relief from the strict discipline of the big company probably encouraged taking liberties. Not that Black wasn't strict. He too had been a Caley man for sixteen years but in a close knit community he couldn't afford to antagonise anyone.

So here's what they did. For a couple of years Norman O'May had been employed as odd-job boy with the company and he was detailed to help Harper shunt his train. After this he would take the tablet down to the office thus letting Harper get home for his tea. On the arrival of the 6.30 he could take a tablet back up to the depot and leave it in the cab. As the summer wore on he too found this cumbersome and prevailed upon Alex Black to let him open the Hall Street instrument with Black's special release key and thus clear the instrument at Lintmill. He could then leave Harper's tablet in the engine and be saved a return walk to the depot. And, after all, everyone knew Harper's engine wouldn't be used again that night.

Things caught up with them on 9 August. The 5.10's guard was in a hurry to be off and left Harper and O'May to stable the train for the night themselves. As on previous occasions, Harper handed the tablet to O'May who opened the points for the depot. Harper propelled his train in but as he passed over the crossing he shouted to O'May to leave the points open as he had to shunt the *Princess* and this would require him to set back on to the main line again. The wee *Princess* was duly drawn out, left up one of the 'lies' and Harper left his engine with a cleaner, G. Jamieson, and trudged off home. O'May meantime went down to the harbour and cleared the Lintmill instrument using Black's key.

Meanwhile at Machrihanish, Jimmy Laing, the driver of the 6.30 was having trouble with a leaky boiler tube and his engine just would not steam. She was so bad that he couldn't even maintain the vacuum and the train brakes were rubbing. Finally he prevailed upon the guard, Willie Black, the superintendent's brother, to pull the pin out on the carriage brakes and thus immobilise them. His ailing engine now managed to start the three-coach train and with between fifty and sixty passengers aboard they set sail for Campbeltown with 'nae brakes'. At Lintmill, the tablet instrument showed the expected 'line clear' and they withdrew the tablet and went on their way. They had a sore problem lifting the train up the hill from Plantation to Tomaig but once over the top they were away. Looking ahead Jimmy saw some children on the line at the rifle range and wound up his hand brake. It had little effect but he whistled twice and Black screwed down the hand brakes on two of the carriages and the speed was reduced to about 10 mph. It was then to his horror Jimmy saw the depot points open. His engine rocked over them on to the depot line and promptly locked its wheels on the wet rails at the water tower. Propelled inexorably onwards by the carriages, Jimmy's locomotive crashed into Hugh Harper's and the cleaner, Jamieson, who was still working on it was killed instantly. As accidents go the impact was slight and only the buffing gear was damaged but in the ensuing Board of Trade enquiry on 2 September the whole story came out. Lt Col Druitt was back for the hearing and strongly condemned the practice which had completely nullified the safety arrangements.

Not that such remonstrations had much effect. Andrew Cunningham was brought up in Low Kilkivan farm and travelled every day to and from Campbeltown on the school train. One afternoon in the early 1920s the school train was waiting in the loop at Lintmill for a train of coals to cross. As it was fine summer weather young Andrew was sitting on the steps of the car having 'got round' the train crew as this was normally prohibited. The coal train appeared from the west and swung over the points into the loop. As it passed the passenger train engine, Andrew saw the coal train's driver fling a lump of coal into the other engine's cab shouting 'there yer tablet, ye can gang oan noo'! The significance of having another fifty tons of similar 'tablets' behind his engine was lost on them.

OPERATING

The passenger timetable varied only slightly throughout the life of the railway. That published in Murrays 1920 timetable was typical : —

Campbeltown & Machrihanish Light

miles		Week Days Only				
		mrn	aft	aft	aft	aft
	Campbeltown dep 10F20		1.20	1e40	4.20	9.43
		Sats			Sats	
6	Machrihanish arr 10F50		1.50	2e10	4.50	10.15

		Week Days Only				
	Machrihanish dep 8d20 11Fo		2.0	2e20	5e10	5.20
		Sats			Sats	
6	Campbeltown arr 8d50 11F30		2.30	2e50	5e40	6.00

Halts at Plantation, Moss Road, Lintmill, Drumlemble, Machrihanish Farm, and Trodigal if required. Special Trains may be arranged for on application at Railway Office.
  d Except Saturdays and School Holidays
  e Except Saturdays
  F Mondays, Wednesdays and Saturdays

Originally the above timetable outdid itself because due to a misprint on the outward section it had 'dep' and 'arr' reversed so the trains were shown to arrive 20 minutes before they left. Even the Campbeltown couldn't manage that.

Other trains were run as the manager thought fit and having local knowledge was more important than having a timetable. For example, trains were run to suit the shifts at the colliery and as this was before the days of pit-head baths, one coach was allocated specifically for this duty. This miners' train and the school train were generally composed of one coach and often worked by one of the o-4-2 engines. The steamer express which connected with the excursion steamer ran non-stop,

Argyll with single coach train

carried no luggage and was usually composed of all six carriages. This necessitated being banked up to Tomaig by whichever 0–6–2 engine was spare. Stephen McCabe, son of the latterday superintendent, used to tell of the times he earned his pocket money by sitting on the front buffer beam of the banker with a leg on either side of the coupler. At the top of the hill he would reach down and lift the chopper which coupled the engine to the last car and thus allow the banking engine to drop back. At holiday weekends, however, the steamer express was cut to five coaches which one engine could manage and the other locomotive worked a one-coach local stopping at all stations. By some slick shunting, the engines changed trains and the local preceded the express home picking up at all stops. In those days there was a football field at the Hungry Hoose and the railway ran specials as far as Plantation crossing whenever games were being played. One of these was specifically mentioned in the *Argyllshire Herald* of 3 February 1912.

The summer that the Territorial Army went to Machrihanish for its summer camp, it of course had to travel on the railway. Troop trains were laid on using every available piece of rolling stock, even trains of empty coal wagons!

When the creamery was opened in Campbeltown, the railway started running a morning milk train, invariably hauled by *Princess*. To augment the railway company's milk wagon, some of the end-door-only coal wagons had side doors cut in their sides. This traffic petered out again once the creamery developed its own road transport which could serve the outlying farms as well.

Not much traffic originated from the farms but on one occasion several small pigs were loaded into the centre van on carriage No 6. On the journey someone opened the communicating door into the van portion and the pigs escaped into the carriage. The train crew stopped the train and the passengers abandoned it speedily followed by the pigs. It took the driver and fireman a good hour to round up everyone, pigs and passengers alike and restore them to their correct places before proceeding on their way.

One piece of regular unpaid freight was an old fishbox. In every small community, there is bound to be a worthy who isn't quite all there. Campbeltown was no exception and this character would fill his fishbox from fish given to him by the fishermen from their boats in the harbour. He then boarded the train with his box and rode free to Machrihanish where he converted his fish to hard cash on highly attractive terms before riding home free to Campbeltown with an empty fishbox and a full pocket. It sometimes pays to be a wee bit gite!

When a ship was loading coal, the necessary siding space at the New Quay was limited. If a ship was due, as much coal as could be carried was stored in the wagon at the Limecraigs siding. To economise on engine power, rakes of coal wagons were run down the cutting by gravity under the control of the wagon handbrakes. At such times an engine would be shunting continually at the harbour and wagons would be shunted along Hall Street to relieve the pressure. This practice was not appreciated by other users of the street. When sufficient empties had accumulated, they would be taken back up the hill in very long trains and reshuffled at the depot for further use.

An unusual working was connected with the painting of the navigation buoys used locally. One of these would be towed into the New Quay and lifted by the coal crane on to a flat wagon (possibly an old hutch carrier) and taken up to the depot. Here the harbour authorities could paint it at their leisure before having it taken back to the quay and popped back in the water.

For the steamer express the tickets were issued on the boat but for all other trains ticket issue was on the train by the guard or conductor and for most of its existence the railway anticipated the airlines by employing pretty girls for this duty. For many years this job befell Nan Galbraith who in the ways of the west became 'Nan o' the train'. When she left the company she was succeeded by young Margaret Leyden, who must have added considerably to the pleasure of travelling on the wee train. Cardboard tickets were issued from ticket racks carried by the conductress and cancelled by a plier type punch. After collecting fares on one coach, the conductress would swing from the lower footsteps of one car to that of the next and continue as before until the entire train load was accounted for. It was best to have this task complete before the train reached Tomaig as the speed was necessarily slow. When all the tickets had been sold, the conductress would signal to the driver if it were required of him to put down at any intermediate stopping places. One of the drivers, Jimmy Ramsay, tells of a time when he was working a single coach train with the old *Chevalier*. Now *Chevalier* had no vacuum brake, so to do this, it was necessary for Ramsay to pull the pin out of the vacuum brake mechanism and thus immobilise the coach's automatic brakes. This wasn't too bad as the engine's handbrake could probably handle one car as well, and in theory, the conductress could use the car's own handbrake. Well, Jimmy was rattling down the hill to the Hungry Hoose when he looked back to get the signal from his conductress of where to stop and there was the car, two lengths behind but gaining fast. Jimmy valued his job and weighed up the chances of catching the car gently or more likely breaking a window or something. Discretion is the better part of valour so Jimmy gave the old *Chevalier* all she'd got and with her wee wheels fair birling he managed to keep ahead of the runaway until it came to rest at the foot of the hill. He then backed up, coupled on and went on his way.

Chevalier came adrift from her train more than once and on another occasion when Margaret Leyden was on duty, the coupling slipped as they were leaving Plantation for Campbeltown. It was a cold wet day and the engine crew huddled in the tiny cab didn't notice they were on their own until they arrived at the harbour. With red faces they backed out of Hall Street and away back over the hill to where Margaret was waiting impatiently with a car load of stranded passengers.

Jimmy Ramsay was aye having runaways of one sort or another. On one occasion when they were drawing coal from the pit, there was a match on at the Plantation football field. Jimmy and his brakesman got into an argument about the rival merits of the two teams as his big Barclay pounded up the hill to Tomaig. Now the Board of Trade had thought fit to insist on the railway having a brake van but the drivers could see no sense in towing a heavy empty vehicle around when by leaving it be they could haul more coal. Jimmy Ramsay had as many wagons as the engine could cope with and his brakesman was travelling on the footplate. At the summit the latter would jump off on to the ballast and drop the wagon brake levers which were arranged on a ratchet and would lock where they were set. But as I said Jimmy was extolling the virtues of his team and failed to notice they were getting near the top. The big 0–6–2 shouldered her train over the Tomaig farm crossing and tore off down the hill on full regulator with her rake swaying out behind her. The violent motion brought the two men back to reality with a jerk and the brakesman jumped down to secure the brakes but found that already the speed was such that it was all he could do to keep up with the train never mind apply brake levers. With the regulator shut and the handbrake wound up tight Jimmy could do no more in the cab so he climbed out over the coal to see what could be done but after a few abortive attempts, it became obvious that to reach the brake levers from the top of the wagon was plain daft. 'Awa back to yer ingin, Jimmy' panted the brakesman, 'and try and haud them'. So Jimmy climbed back over the coal to his rapidly accelerating engine. The brakesman was soon left far behind as the runaway gathered speed down the hill.

Past the sheds they rushed and down through the cutting. Jimmy opened the whistle as they approached the Kilkerran Road and they shot over the ungated crossing. Across the quarry green they roared but on the flat the engine's twenty-two tons could 'haud' them and they slid to a standstill in Hall Street with about fifty feet of track left between them and the Royal Hotel.

Another time he nearly repeated the 1910 disaster (how were the points again set for the depot?) but his engine derailed quietly into a pile of ashes. And various carriers' carts carried the marks of Jimmy's buffers picked up in Hall Street.

When Jimmy Ramsay retired from the railway he landed a job at the old picture house (by that time the *Rex*, a much bigger one, had also been built in Hall Street) and worked within the scene of his earlier exploits for many years. Many's the visitor who went to the wee picture house to hear about the wee train rather than to see the film!

One of the fitters and spare-time drivers was Willie Butters who came from the Highland Railway in 1906 in the days when Peter Drummond was locomotive superintendent. He was very fond of the small engines, especially *Princess*. He could tune her Stephenson valve gear till she ran like a sewing machine. When it came to *Argyll* and *Atlantic*'s Walschaerts gear though, he was sorely puzzled and, as he himself said, 'I jist put it back where ah foon it'. Willie's career with the railway came to an abrupt end when he let *Princess*'s water go low and burnt the firebox crown. Edward McCabe, the superintendent, sacked him on the spot but Willie was more troubled about the damage to *Princess* than the loss of his job. *Princess* never worked again. Willie Butters stayed on in the town but such is the way of these parts that fifty years later he was still an 'incomer'. The 1923 grouping and the 1948 nationalisation passed Willie by, and shortly before his death a few years ago the Highland and Peter Drummond were to him still on the go!

The c & m had its share of minor accidents. On 14 January 1908, a cold windy day, a fisherman named William Gilchrist was making his way across the Quarry Green and following the course of the railway. He was going to the Doirlinn Bank, the name given to the shingle bar connecting Davaar Island to the shore, to gather mussels, and for this purpose was carrying a basket. He had just reached the gap in the wall on to the Kilkerran Road when he was overtaken by the train which he had failed to notice. The engine struck him a glancing blow but his clothing or his basket got entangled with the engine and he was dragged across the road and into the cutting before falling clear, luckily outwards. He escaped with bruises and internal injuries.

The driver, William Brown, was charged with reckless driving and failing to keep a good lookout. In his defence he said that he was observing the 5 mph speed limit and had sounded his engine's whistle on approaching the crossing although not obliged to do so. He had been on the right hand side of the cab from which he had had a good view of the line ahead but just at the crossing he had crossed over to the other side. He had seen no one until he heard the guard William Black blowing his whistle and immediately pulled up. Only then did he see Gilchrist lying beside the track. His defence was not accepted and he was fined £1 with the option of seven days' imprisonment.

In May the same year a man was found injured at the crossing place at Moss Road.

On 24 July 1909, the postman was driving his high spring cart over the level crossing at Trodigal in a sleepy mood and failed to notice the approaching train. The resulting collision did more damage to His Majesty's mail gig than to the train.

In August 1917, two engines were in collision at the sheds and were sufficiently badly damaged that some trains had to be cancelled until repairs were effected.

During Easter 1920 a youth by the name of William Paterson was playing about the coaches at Machrihanish when he slipped and the carriage wheel severed his foot. More serious was the accident in September 1921 when a man fell off the train and was killed. He had been riding on the platform and lost his balance. Of course regulations were enforced for a bit and two months later a fisherman named John Mackenzie was charged with boarding the train while it was in motion. After this warning notices were painted on the end white panel of each coach.

WEATHER

The Kintyre weather is typical of that found on the West Coast, often wet but seldom extreme. An exception to this ruling was January 1915 when a storm of great intensity raged over the west of Scotland. The normally sheltered waters of Campbeltown Loch were whipped to a frenzy and an exceptionally high tide caused the waves to dash over the retaining wall of the Quarry Green. The railway was soon buried in debris and the ballast disturbed sufficiently to make the track unsafe. Until the flotsam could be cleared and the rails realigned, the town terminus became the Kilkerran Crossing and passengers were entrained there.

On another occasion a combination of high tides, heavy rain and a westerly wind caused the Machrihanish water to rise to an unprecedented height. It rose so far that it flooded the adjacent railway and a passenger train from Campbeltown met a minor loch in its path. The driver decided to risk it and proceeded slowly into the flood but it was deeper than he thought. Narrow gauge trains are notoriously low slung and as the engine paddled out into the water, the level rose around it until it reached the fire grate where with an explosive hiss it doused the fire. The driver tried to keep going on what steam he had but the going was too hard and the train stalled with only its last carriage on dry ground. And the water was still rising!

The other big engine was at Machrihanish and separated from the stranded train by the rest of the flood. Only the old *Chevalier* was available at Limecraigs and she was cold. Moreover only the superintendent, Edward McCabe and 'Nan o' the trains' were on duty and while McCabe got some rescue tackle together, Nan endeavoured to lay a fire and get steam up in the old engine. Between them they coaxed life into the aged machine and with 60 lbs on the clock set off into the storm to rescue the stranded train. The old *Chevalier* lived up to its name and pulled the other train back on to dry land again.

February 1929 brought one of those heavy blizzards that paralyse the countryside and bring all transport to a standstill. Kintyre usually misses these snow storms but this time it got fair snowed up. It took the Campbeltown railway a week to dig itself out. The railway is reputed to have had a sheet iron

The first train through, 1929

snowplough but a photograph published in a Glasgow paper on 19 February showed the first train for a week passing through roof-high walls of snow. The train consisted of one coach and an 0–6–2 engine propelling what looks like a coal wagon.

RAILWAY STAFF

The C & M did not of course employ the same number of people all the time but nineteen or twenty persons were usual until the last year or so. There were three platelayers, seven train staff, one full-time station clerk with a part-time assistant.

The balance was made up by various casual employees who came and went by the season as demand varied.

The first superintendent was Alex Black whose brother William was also employed as guard and assistant superintendent. Black was followed by Edward McCabe in 1915. McCabe was there to the end except for 1929 when for that year only the superintendent is recorded as one P. Gillespie. 'Wee McCabe', as he was called, used his own growing family to augment the dwindling staff when strict economies were being practised after the colliery closed down. The superintendent was the only company employee to be issued with a uniform but conductress Margaret Leyden wore a dark gaberdine raincoat and beret purchased at her own expense.

On a remote railway like the c & m, the employees had to be fairly versatile, especially the superintendent who turned his hand to most jobs not normally associated with his office. It was not unusual to find McCabe under an engine adjusting brake rigging or setting valve gear.

CHAPTER SIX

Decline and Fall

RIVALS TO THE RAILWAY

The Campbeltown & Machrihanish Light Railway killed the horse charabanc traffic stone dead on the steamer excursion service. Horse-drawn brakes still operated on the Southend service and on the Tarbert Royal Mail run. The Tarbert mail coach was a very fine equipage carrying passengers inside and out and drawn by two immaculate horses. In 1913 the first tottering steps of a new infant were taken, the Argyllshire Motor Company, which started operating Commer buses on the Tarbert run from Campbeltown. The first casualty was the horse-drawn mail coach. The Great War stopped further developments and the motor company was reduced to running Ford vans and eventually gave up. Their run was immediately taken over by two concerns, Mr Duncan Ramsay who ran a garage, and Messrs Craig Brothers also a garage firm. In 1923 they were followed by A. & P. McConnachie who secured the mail contract. Competition between the bus companies was severe and cut-throat. Ramsay disappeared from the scene but the Craigs and McConnachies fought it out, racing each other from stage to stage. The two firms carried different coloured lights at night for their loyal passengers to identify them. In the late 1920s both had begun to operate a service from Campbeltown to Machrihanish in direct competition to the railway company. The Campbeltown Coal Company had never quite recovered from either the coal strikes of the 1920s or from the speculation which had reduced its working capital to almost nil. Again, Campbeltown coal wasn't the best and with mounting depression in industry those coal users left could be selective. The coal company ceased production in 1929 and the railway was left to fend for itself on passenger traffic. Without bus competition this would have been difficult but with the charabancs loading passengers on the Old Quay itself, the wee train only got what was left. Still the train could show a clean pair of heels and for through passengers it was faster and more comfortable than the buses. Having the right of way, if the train reached Plantation first it was bound to be at Machrihanish before any of the buses so it was 'first to the Hungry Hoose' that got the next day's custom! Some of the speeds *Argyll* and *Atlantic* put up in those last years would have appalled the Board of Trade. By observing strict economy the railway was still viable and at a shareholders meeting in 1929, although it was announced that receipts were down £352 19s 5d, operating expenses were down by £831 1s 1d. A balance had been brought forward of £119 10s 6d from the previous year and was increased to £484 9s 8d.

The McConnachies and West Coast Motors, as the Craigs were now known, discounted the railways' operations and divided their routes up between themselves. When the new Road Traffic Act was passed McConnachies applied for a licence to operate the Machrihanish service which was successfully opposed by the C & M L R. On the axiom if you can't fight them,

MacConnachie's bus on the Old Quay

join them, the c & m bought two red Reo Speedwagon buses
and put them on to augment its train service. It then tried to
run them to Southend as well but was blocked by McConnachie
who already had a licence for this run. The buses of course
served Drumlemble and other villages much more intimately
than the railway but the Reos were very unreliable and were
always breaking down. The train ran the summer excursion
traffic in 1931 but when traffic dwindled in the autumn,
McCabe ran the buses more and more. After two months of
idleness the passenger train started running early in 1932 in
anticipation of the summer steamer traffic. It was soon found
however that all was far from well with the engines. Although
spares had been purchased as late as July 1930, expensive
repairs would be required. When the summer sailings started
in May there was no whistle from the wee train to greet the
turbine's arrival; the railway had died.

THE END OF THE RAILWAY

The railway sold its goodwill, and more important, its
passenger transport licence rights, to the McConnachies for
£1,000 and began to systematically dispose of its capital assets.
A chartered accountant, Mr H. E. Hill Louden was appointed
liquidator at an extraordinary meeting of the shareholders on
21 November 1933, with instructions to wind up the affairs
of the company. The periodical *Punch* made capital out of it
with the quip ' "Scottish light railway to be wound up", who
found McKey?'

On 3 May 1934, James N. Connel Ltd, the scrap merchant of
Coatbridge, bought the railway's plant and rolling stock and
the land reverted to the Duke of Argyll. The six carriages were
sold locally as holiday huts and on 11 July the first of these
was transferred by road from the railway sheds at Limecraigs
to Trench Point on the other side of Campbeltown Loch. The
carriage fought to the end; it was 4 am on the Wednesday
before it was finally settled at the Trench.

The scrap men moved in smartly, although some dismantling
mainly of colliery track had started the preceding December.
Within a fortnight *Argyll* and *Chevalier* were no more, and
by May the lifting of the rails had progressed as far as the

Page 95 *Makers' pictures of* (above) *Atlantic*; (right) Princess (*Skylark class*); (below) Chevalier

Page 96 (above left) *Coach No 1 in Pickering's yard*; (above right) *Coach No 6*; (below left) *large coal wagon and milk wagon*; (below right) *Brake van*

vicinity of Kintyre Park. *Atlantic* was put into steam and one of the railway's drivers, Davey Lindsay, was taken on by Connel to drive her on the demolition train. All through the summer *Atlantic* chuffed up and down the rapidly dwindling track and in the middle of August she made her last journey to the New Quay to be dismantled.

The bones of the engines were shipped in the puffer *Norman* to Irvine for dispatch to the steelworks for melting down.

SURVIVING REMAINS

By the following year only the rails on the New Quay were left. A few wagons remained on the pier for a while and were used for odd jobs loading or unloading vessels. The rails also remained in level crossings at Kilkerran Road and Plantation Crossing; in fact they remain to this day at Plantation but are now 18 in under the road surface though they poke out through the grass on the west side of the carriageway. The sleepers were piled up in an enormous untidy heap at the depot and were used later to reinforce the butts on the rifle range until that too followed the Railway into limbo. The roof of the carriage shed has been used on a garage building at the old coal ree in Argyll Street but divided and now used over two bays.

The harbour background has not changed much but Hall Street is now a dual carriageway. Quarry Green is a municipal putting green and the cutting has been surfaced by the town council as a footpath. At the top of the cutting the depot triangle lay derelict for many years but in recent times the site was levelled to form a playing field. Between here and the summit, housing developments have obliterated the course of the line but from there on the roadbed can be traced without too much difficulty. The Machrihanish station area sprouted prefabs after the war and these in turn have given way to more permanent houses.

Atlantic's whistle no longer hoots in Hall Street but rests peacefully in the museum of the Campbeltown Library in front of which it once paused so often.

F

CHAPTER SEVEN

Rolling Stock

The rolling stock used on the C & M L R was both unusual and distinctive. All the vehicles were supplied new and none was sold out of service for use on other lines. The coal traffic especially deserves mention. The early wagons provide an almost unique example of narrow gauge transporter wagons carrying even smaller narrow gauge vehicles (the only other case known to the author was the Padarn Railway in North Wales, but there the transporter wagons were 4 ft 0 in gauge). The later coal wagons were an interesting parallel with main line practice wherein a large fleet of private owner wagons was worked by the public railway company.

The passenger trains too were unusual. The carriages were an interesting mixture of railway and tramway practice with a touch of the American mid-west thrown in. The trains had a uniformity of appearance rare on narrow gauge lines and uncommon even on standard gauge railways until recent years.

LOCOMOTIVES

Pioneer

This first locomotive is somewhat of an enigma. It was delivered by the steamer *Kintyre* on 11 November 1877. The maker is unknown and no photograph or drawing has been found to give an idea of its appearance.

It has been described as a well-tank locomotive and had inside frames. As delivered it was an 0–4–0WT with a 4 ft coupled wheelbase and weighed about nine tons. The driving wheels were 24 in diameter. The cylinders were 6 in x 10 in. To correct the uneven riding as an 0–4–0WT a trailing pony truck with 15 in diameter wheels was added.

Maintenance on *Pioneer* was difficult. Her inside frames necessitated the grate and lower part of the firebox being very narrow to be accommodated within the available space. The upper part of the firebox was widened out to suit the diameter of the boiler and give sufficient area of tubeplate. The result of this construction was that when the firebox had to be renewed, it could only be removed by first taking out the end of the boiler. This operation entailed a great deal of work that would otherwise have been unnecessary. Once other locomotives had appeared, this difficulty probably hastened *Pioneer*'s demise.

Pioneer was not incorporated in C & M L R stock in 1906 as by that time she was stored out of use at the colliery.

Chevalier

In 1883, Messrs J. & T. L. Galloway purchased from Messrs Andrew Barclay & Co of Kilmarnock an attractive 0–4–0 saddle tank named *Chevalier*. It was their works No 269 and was destined to be the longest lived Campbeltown engine.

When delivered, *Chevalier* was a much bigger machine than her predecessor but had the same 4 ft wheelbase and 24 in driving wheels. A big improvement was her outside frames which allowed for a more reasonable firebox. *Chevalier* was fitted with a stove-pipe chimney atop a large ogee saddle tank which extended from the smokebox front over the boiler but the space above the firebox was clear except for a monumental combined dome and safety valve. The original cab was high and had sidesheets which swept forward at the lower front to embrace two small coal bunkers on either side of the firebox. The back of the cab was completely open and the crew were protected by a waist high handrail.

The screw handbrake operated wooden brake blocks on the rear driving wheels only. A sandbox was provided on the right footplate and delivered sand between the driving wheels.

Wooden buffer beams were augmented by large wooden blocks which extended from slightly above footplate level to three inches above the rails. The coupling consisted of a lug and shackle.

The springs were carried above the footplate and were of the leaf pattern when delivered. During the first twenty years of the locomotive's existence these were replaced by heavy

Chevalier at the Colliery, 1900

coil springs with a crossbar to mate with the original hangers.

When delivered, the locomotive was ornately lined out but the colour scheme has not survived the mists of time. Cast brass nameplates were fixed to the saddle tank and the maker's plate on the cab side bore the legend 'A. Barclay & Son, Engineers, Kilmarnock No 269 1883'.

The first major modification to *Chevalier* was like *Pioneer* the fitting of a pony truck under the cab, as her long overhangs and short wheelbase were aggravating the imperfections of the track. This was found to be a great improvement in preventing damage to the permanent way and at the same time adding to the comfort of the enginemen. The pony truck was free to follow the curves of the track and had several inches lateral movement. Attachment was by a long radius bar centred under the trailing coupled axle. The total wheelbase was now 8 ft 9 in.

Chevalier's fortunes waned when *Princess* arrived in 1900 and even more so in 1966 when the big 0–6–2Ts arrived. However, with the demand for coal, even Machrihanish coal, during the First World War *Chevalier* was overhauled and emerged unrecognisable. Gone was her curvaceous cab. Instead a new one was fashioned similar to the Kerr Stuart one on *Princess*. This was accomplished by taking the existing spectacle plate and moving it forward to the rear of the saddle tank. The two sidesheets were bolted to their opposite sides such that the former leading edge became the cab cut-out. Sheet metal completed the cab which now had a back and a small extended bunker. The bunker overhung the wooden buffer beam so a further beam of wood was added. The big dumb buffers were replaced by spring side buffers and Norwegian centre couplers. A rather handsome capped chimney replaced the original stovepipe one. From this time on she was listed on the railway company's books in the annual returns, although she had in fact been transferred with *Princess*.

In her rebuilt form *Chevalier* proved to be a better engine than *Princess* and in the early 1920s when *Princess* could no longer work, cannibalisation took place. One of *Princess*'s boiler mounted sandboxes was fitted to *Chevalier*'s left front footplate with an operating rod back to the cab. Cylinder lubricators, injectors (in the firebox waterlegs) and other details followed. Shorn of her brass name and maker's plates no one could describe her as beautiful but she nevertheless had the charm of an ugly duckling.

Chevalier survived to the end, a life of fifty years, but in her last days she worked very little as the closing of the colliery had removed her *raison d'être*. Never much suited to passenger working she spent her life hauling and shunting coal and her tinny off-beat exhaust enabled her to be identified from afar. Her top speed was 15 mph and it was possible for the youth of Campbeltown to race her from the New Quay to Kilkerran Crossing and win.

Princess

Messrs Kerr Stuart of Stoke-on-Trent, like Barclays', were prominent in the field of industrial and narrow gauge engines. One of their standard classes was an 0–4–2 side tank engine known as their *Skylark* class. These engines were built in batches and held in stock in a forward state of construction until a purchaser was found. Different gauges from 2 ft 0 in to

Princess at the Colliery, 1900

over 3 ft 6 in were accommodated by fitting the wheels inside or outside the frames as required. Many of these wee engines were built and some were still running around after the Second World War.

No 717 of 1900 was purchased by the Campbeltown Coal Company and delivered within seven weeks. She was named *Princess* in deference to the Duke of Argyll's bride, Queen Victoria's daughter Princess Louise, and carried her name painted on her tanks. If the first two engines were quaint, *Princess* was a caricature. All the essential features of a proper locomotive were there but on so small an engine everything was out of proportion. Her overall cab towered over her slim boiler. The tiny bunker was so narrow that if a lump of coal got stuck in it a long bar was the only thing to get it clear. Having a pony truck from the start, her coupled wheelbase was incredibly short at 3 ft 0 in. How she bucked along!

Her driving wheels were 2 ft 3 in and the pony wheels 1 ft 4½ in while her total wheelbase was 7 ft 8 in.

The dome and safety valves were mounted on the raised firebox crown inside the cab and her sand was carried in two domes on the boiler where it would be warm and dry. She was the first Campbeltown engine to carry spring buffers.

Princess was taken into C & M L R stock in 1906 and fitted with vacuum brake equipment for working passenger trains. She was often used for working the single winter coach and other light duties. One of these was the daily milk train that ran for some years.

But she didn't have the lasting powers of the Barclay and when her firebox was done so was she. She was shunted to the end of the line next to the engine shed and lay there for years gradually losing her fittings to her older stablemate. Her ultimate disposal is unknown but she was not listed as extant when the railway company was wound up.

Argyll

With the inaugural passenger service, the new railway company ordered from Andrew Barclay Sons & Co a large 0-6-2 side-tank loco No 1049 of 1906. This engine was much bigger than anything Campbeltown had known previously and must have seemed enormous on the two foot three. The six-coupled wheelbase was 6 ft 4 in with a total wheelbase of 12 ft 9 in. Her driving wheels were 2 ft 9 in and her radial truck wheels 1 ft 10 in. The cylinders were 11½ in diameter by 18 in stroke. With a full complement of 600 gallons of water and 15 cwt of coal, the locomotive weighed 20 tons 10 cwt. She was a powerful engine and could handle 70 ton trains although normally she was restricted to 42 tons.

Like the previous engines, no number was carried but the name *Argyll* was emblazoned in block gold letters on the side tanks. Forward of the name was the crest of the company and on the other side Barclays' distinctive oval builders plate.

Argyll was an outside-framed outside-cylinder engine with the drive to the rear coupled wheels. Another departure from the previous engines was the use of Walschaerts valve gear, which sorely puzzled at least some of the fitters who were required to adjust it. The footplate angle was raised over the cylinders and valve gear and the large side tanks were similarly shaped. The elegant Barclay cab and bunker set off the rather massive appearance of the engine. The boiler carried a large dome surmounted by two safety valves and two large cast iron sandboxes operated by a lever from the cab. A shapely capped chimney was carried on the smokebox.

The locomotive was fitted with vacuum brake equipment and Norwegian centre buffer couplings. Throughout her life *Argyll* was also fitted with conventional spring side buffers on wooden blocks, for working chain coupled wagons. The maker's photograph does not show these but they were fitted either before delivery or immediately after, and certainly before the engine went into service. A small detail, but one essential for identification, was the shape of her buffer beams. The cut-outs on the lower corners of the front beam were radiused, while on the rear one they were straight. Side safety chains were provided but seldom carried.

Argyll lived through her life with few changes. The lamp brackets on the smokebox and cab back were lowered to the footplate and bunker back respectively. The big square spectacle plates proved a nuisance when coal was piled in the bunker, so the lower half of the rear windows was closed off by a plate. Apart from growing steadily older and eventually decrepit, *Argyll* remained unaltered.

Atlantic

In 1907 the company purchased their last locomotive from Andrew Barclay Sons & Co, an 0–6–2 side tank No 1098, identical to *Argyll*. So similar were the two engines that it was difficult to tell them apart. The only structural difference was *Atlantic*'s rear buffer beam, which had radiused cut-outs like her front buffer beam. She too was not built with side buffers, but received them immediately after. Rumour has it that *Argyll* and *Atlantic* shared the same set of four buffers for a few months in 1907, but this has never been substantiated by photographs.

Atlantic was always a better steamer than *Argyll* and had the distinction of being the last engine to steam on the line. She was used by Connel on the demolition train in 1934. Her whistle and gauge glass are now in the museum section of the Campbeltown Free Library.

Atlantic was highly regarded by her makers and appeared in several Barclay catalogues as Class P. Her description and photo in a Spanish issue carrying the exotic caption 'Locomotora Para Lineas Sub-Urbanas, Y Ferrocarriles de via Estrecha' were a far cry indeed from the peninsula of Kintyre. With her sister, *Atlantic* was the typical Campbeltown engine, and after 1906 most of the work, passenger and coal, was done by them.

CARRIAGES

To cater for the forthcoming passenger service Messrs R. Y. Pickering & Co of Wishaw were asked to tender for carriages suitable for use on the new service. This company submitted three possibilities: a cross bench covered bogie car with open sides and tip over seats, a similar car with fixed seats facing each other in pairs, and an enclosed saloon carriage with end balconies and steps to ground level. All these proposals had tramway type curved sheet iron dashes. Indeed the two cross bench cars resembled coastal tramway practice on many electric systems, which practice survives to this day on the summer cars on the Manx Electric Railway. All these were 43 ft 6 in long and were carried on two 4 ft 0 in wheelbase bogies at 30 ft 0 in centres.

After perusing these proposals, the railway company asked Pickerings to modify the proposed design of saloon coach and eventually an order was placed for four of these vehicles. They were delivered by sea early in the summer of 1906.

The four new carriages, appropriately number 1 to 4 were among the finest passenger vehicles ever to run on so narrow a gauge. A considerable improvement on the match board sided version originally proposed, these carriages were long, rakish and beautifully proportioned.

Each saloon had eight large plate glass windows in which every second one had a tip-in 'hopper' light. A centre gangway ran from end to end, flanked by '2 and 2' swing back wooden seats following tramway practice. Sixty-four persons were carried in each coach. Entrance was by hinged doors in each end bulkhead, there being another bulkhead in the centre of the coach. The centre bulkhead was solid but the end bulkheads had a window on either side of the door. The end platforms had two steps to road level at each side. In place of the original proposal for sheet iron dashes, ornate wrought iron

Coach interior

railings were provided. When running, each platform could be closed by telescopic trellis gates at the top of the steps, although these were seldom used. The high curved roof was domed at each end over the balcony. Panelling of the period was used to finish the sides and ends of the body. The body was of wood but was carried on a steel underframe mounted on two diamond frame bogies.

Norwegian centre buffer couplers and side chains were fitted and the vehicles were equipped with vacuum brake. A hand-brake column at each end, acting on the adjacent bogie, could be used to supplement the vacuum brake and for parking. Contemporary 1906 writings state that the lighting was by candles. This may have been in error as acetylene gas lighting was used from very early on. The coaches had no roof vent-ilators when delivered and the fitting of these in 1907 may give a clue to the fitting of gas lighting. The gas generators were carried under the floor between the truss rods.

The first four carriages were followed in 1907 by coach No 5 which at first glance would appear identical to Nos 1 to 4. However No 5 was the mirror image of the first four. Looking side on to No 5, the extreme left hand window was plain, while the extreme right hand had a hopper ventilator. Perhaps the carriage builder read the drawing wrongly!

The final coach No 6 had the same general house style as the others but had a central luggage compartment flanked by three-window saloons at each end. The luggage compartment had normal railway type double hinged doors on one side only. Two panels separated these doors from the windows and on the plain side there were eight panels. A normal railway drop light was provided in the left hand door.

Unlike the first five vehicles the opening windows in No 6's saloons slid downwards to open and two iron bars prevented people from hanging out of the larger opening. No 6 had roof ventilators from new and the others were brought into line soon after.

Occasionally No 6 got herself turned on the triangle and caused consternation in Hall Street when all the luggage had to be carried round the end of the train. As No 6 was often the middle vehicle of the train, many were the curses.

One coach was designated the miners' coach, generally the one most in need of overhaul but in summer all six ran as a rake on the steamer express.

The carriages survived the closure of the railway for nearly as long as they had worked on it. In June 1934 they were transported to the disused shipyard at Trench Point, on the other side of Campbeltown Loch and there used as holiday huts. Placed in lines of three and two with one at right angles at the entrance, they still contrived to look like trains. For a while they kept their original colours and formed a landmark for miles.

The Admiralty occupied Trench Point during the 1939-45 war and painted them black all over, with boarded-up windows. When peace returned, the navy pulled out and the carriages gradually disintegrated under the combined efforts of the weather, the tinkers and the vandals. By August 1958 only the underframes were left and they disappeared soon after. Before everything vanished, two of the wrought iron railings were rescued and now form part of the author's stairway. In 1969 wrought iron is again fashionable!

C C C COAL WAGONS

Early Stock

The original wagons used on the 1876 line were probably merely mine hutches. The dumb buffers originally fitted to *Chevalier* were too deep to mate only with the later known wagons. These early hutches or trams would not be designed for protracted running and would give constant trouble by derailing, bearing failure and such like.

By 1902 there had been in use for some years eighteen flat four wheeled wagons which carried four mine hutches transversely. A detailed description of these survives in T. Lindsay Galloway's paper read to the Students of the Institution of Civil Engineers in 1902 : —

> The wagons are all of the platform type, having short rails laid transversely on which the small wagons or trams containing the coal are carried. Each railway wagon carries four mine wagons containing about 9½ cwt of coal. It may appear that there is a considerable proportion of tare or dead weight to be hauled by such an arrangement, but it is not really so defective as it seems, as the following figures will show : —
>
> | | cwt |
> | ---------------------- | --- |
> | Weight of railway wagon | 18 |
> | Four trams | 10 |
> | Coal | 38 |
> | | — |
> | | 66 |
>
> The useful load is thus 57½ per cent of the gross. The system has the advantage of saving breakage of coal, and of facility in loading and unloading; but it probably would not be adopted if the plant were to be redesigned at the present day.
>
> The wagons have a wheelbase of 4 ft 6 in. The wheels are 24 in in diameter, of chilled iron, forced on steel axles by hydraulic pressure. These chilled iron wheels are found to be exceedingly durable. Each wagon is provided with a hand brake, which can be fastened down when required.

These wagons had dumb buffers formed by extending the solebars and were fitted with chain couplings.

The late D. McDougall, who was a joiner at the pit, recalls that each wagon had a 5 in by 2 in beam locked with pins to hold the hutches steady. This was not entirely successful as they occasionally spilled off. Mr McDougall believes some of the flat wagons were fitted with sides and made into conventional $3\frac{1}{2}$ ton wagons. This seems a likely thing to do but no photographic evidence has so far been unearthed.

Mr A. Cunningham who spent his boyhood at Low Kilkivan Farm remembers one of these wagons at the colliery as late as 1918.

1904–6 Proposals

The Campbeltown Coal Co approached Messrs R. Y. Pickering of Wishaw for various suggestions aimed at speeding the handling of coal, when the proposed new railway company was formed.

Pickerings produced a series of proposed wagons whose inspiration sprang from the early hutch carriers and it may have been intended to use the existing underframes.

The first proposal embodied a steel body whose floor consisted of a longitudinal inverted 'V'. Upward opening doors were fitted the entire length of each side. The end of each underframe was semicircular and a single link coupled them together. Lifting brackets were provided to enable the wagon's load to be discharged when suspended by a crane over a ship's hold. The door catch could be operated remotely by a rope.

The second proposal was for a similar vehicle but the steel body was purely a box with end-doors and it was clipped to an underframe similar to the existing hutch wagons. The wagon would have had dumb buffers and chain couplings and if built, would have been an early example of container traffic.

The third proposal was much more elaborate and comprised a hopper body on a steel underframe. The body would have been suspended from a crane and the bottom doors open to allow the load to discharge. The body was arranged to rest on an angle iron cradle in such a manner that no other locking was necessary.

The drawings of these three wagon types are all dated 1904 but two years later a conventional narrow gauge hopper wagon was proposed. This wagon would have had dumb buffers and 3-link couplings and would have been similar to dozens running on the Winchburgh tramway, four of which are now on the Talyllyn Railway.

None of these schemes seem to have progressed beyond the drawing board and in each case the vehicles probably represented too high a capital investment.

$3\frac{1}{4}$ ton Coal Wagons

The coal company decided to 'cut their coat according to their cloth' and purchased a large quantity of conventional wooden coal trucks with end-doors at one end. These were 5 planked and had dumb buffers and chain couplings. From a study of surviving photographs the axleboxes appear to be fitted with a single coil spring between the box and the frame.

Some at least of these wagons, and probably all of them, were built by Hurst Nelson Ltd of Motherwell and carried HN plates on the solebar. A search through the Hurst Nelson photographs, however, has failed to produce any further evidence. These photographs are lodged in the Motherwell Public Library but are not necessarily complete. More surprising was the finding of two drawings of these wagons in R. Y. Pickering's records. Both drawings are sketchy and may have been drawn from the HN vehicles by a draughtsman who wished to have a record for internal use. One of the Pickering sketches shows a comparison between a $3\frac{1}{4}$ ton and a $4\frac{1}{2}$ ton wagon, each having the same underframe and brake gear. This underframe differs from that shown on photographs of actual wagons.

$4\frac{1}{2}$ ton Coal Wagons

Later wagons supplied to the coal company were of larger capacity having 6-plank sides and were slightly wider and longer. Leaf springs were provided on the axleboxes and as well as dumb buffers, Norwegian centre buffer couplers were used. To couple these wagons to earlier stock, the pin for the Norwegian hook was drawn out, the hook removed and a chain substituted and secured by the same pin. At each end a socket for carrying the Norwegian hooks was provided halfway up the body planking.

The big wagons generally ran as a complete rake to avoid the coupling problem, but in the 1920s it was found convenient to marshal one big wagon at each end of a rake of $3\frac{1}{4}$ tonners to facilitate rapid coupling of the locomotives. By this time only the 0–6–2Ts retained their side buffers and by the high polish on them it was evident that they seldom contacted anything harder than a cleaning rag.

Again Pickerings have two drawings of this type, one a very detailed one and carrying an enquiry number but no date. This firm however, can find no record of having built any of these wagons although their second drawing agrees with photographs to the smallest rivet detail. One can only presume that the enquiry drawing was passed to a competitor who saw no reason to change it.

Some of the end-door wagons had side doors cut in them to enable them to be used for pit-props, mining gear etc and also by the railway company for merchandise.

In an inventory dated 6 January 1922, 150 railway wagons are listed valued at £750.

Half a dozen trucks were still marooned on the truncated track on the New Quay in 1935. The rest had already been cut up on site.

C & M L R WAGONS

The railway company in its annual returns claimed the grand total of two goods wagons. This borders on the absurd but seems nevertheless to be true. The coal company's wagons were used by the railway company as and when capacity was required.

Brake Van

The Board of Trade were not at all happy at the prospect of loaded coal trains descending a 1 in 35 gradient with a public road crossing and a street terminus at the foot, especially as these coal trains had to rely on the engine's brakes and their own handbrakes. A brake van was insisted on.

The railway company approached Messrs R. Y. Pickering & Co who proposed a neat 7 ton brake van with open end platforms of typical appearance. The railway company were sufficiently impressed to place an order with Pickerings in 1909, but if a brake van was necessary it should be capable of other uses too. The final design differed considerably from the original and was more of a goods van with brakes.

The 'big van' as it was known, was a box van with outside

timbering and sliding doors at opposite ends of each side. Cast iron weights were set into pockets under the floor to give it drag and a central handbrake column applied two brake shoes to each wheel. Sanding was also provided from internal sandboxes. Like the locos, spring side buffers and side chains were supplied in addition to the Norwegian centre couplers.

The engine crews soon found out that this juggernaut was equal to at least a couple of loaded wagons over the top at Tomaig and when things were busy, one brake van couldn't be on all the trains that were running, so why should it be on any? The big van was seldom used and certainly not on the job she was built for. For years she lay at the end of the spur at Machrihanish station and never turned a wheel.

Milk Wagon

The other wagon, believed to have been built by Pickerings, was used for milk traffic (in conjunction with modified coal wagons) and for the general carriage of goods. It was sometimes attached to the 'local' passenger trains and had centre couplers to match the carriages. Like the 4½ ton coal wagons it had sockets at each end for the spare 'chopper' for the couplers. The milk wagon had low planked sides surmounted by two open spars to give additional height.

A Pickering enquiry drawing of December 1907 shows a similar wagon but without the spar extensions to the sides. This may or may not be the same vehicle but there is no record of its being supplied by the Wishaw company. The story may well be the same as that outlined for the big coal wagons.

Snow Plough

The railway company also possessed a sheet iron snow plough which could be fastened to the front of a locomotive. However, a photograph published in the Glasgow *Bulletin* on 19 February 1929, shows the first train through after five days of snow blockage propelling a coal wagon.

Linesman's Trolley

The platelaying gang had a light bogie for maintenance work. This was frequently used by late night revellers in Campbeltown to return to Drumlemble after the last train had gone. Once pushed to the summit at Tomaig they could toboggan down to Plantation Crossing and either walk along the road or propel the bogie by punting with a long pole on the level stretch home.

COLOUR SCHEMES

No record has survived of the colours of the early locomotives although *Chevalier* was lined out in an elaborate manner when built, and still showed the lining in 1900. *Princess* was lined out in the standard Kerr Stuart manner and the lining was still visible as she lay derelict in 1925.

Argyll and *Atlantic* were described by the makers as being painted olive green and lined out in vermilion, black and yellow. Contemporary writing in 1906 gives *Argyll* as being painted 'exactly as the North British Railway engines'. The F. Moore painting on the frontispiece shows the engine in a similar livery to that of the N B R. None of the engines seem to have been repainted at any time although the two big engines were polished so much that the undercoat showed through on the buffer beams. Most people remember the engines as black but many comment on the lining which also shows on the very last photographs.

The coaches were described in 1906 as being olive green and white, or merely green and white, and F. Moore's painting shows them green and white. Roofs were white initially but soon became dark 'roof colour'. The author has a piece of coach moulding which had been covered all its life by the iron work of the gate and this fragment is green, something similar to the British Railways light multiple-unit green of the early 1960s. However, more than half the people who knew the railway describe the coaches as brown and cream. Coloured photographs of the period have the cars tinted brown and white and this may be correct, but these tinted postcards are notoriously inaccurate. Whether the carriages were green or brown or if both, when the change took place, will probably never be proved now. The body colour was continued on the moulding round the white panels. The car numbers, 1 to 5, were carried under the windows at each end and the initials 'C & M L Ry' carried in the centre. No 6 started life with the

G

initials at the ends and 'No 6' on either side of the centre doors. 'Guard' and 'Luggage' was carried on the two doors. Later the number was shifted to the end panels as on the other five and the initials appeared twice, nearer the centre

The goods brake van was painted green as new and lettered 'No I C & M L Ry'. For some reason, Pickerings did not put a dot after the 'C' on any of the vehicles, although the coaches at least acquired them later. They also persisted in the 'Ry' abbreviation for Railway.

The hutch wagons seem to have been unlettered, but may have carried a number. The two sizes of coal wagon were painted grey but were generally badly soiled with coal dust. New planks were put in and left unpainted, as happened also on the standard gauge in recent years. The letters 'C C C' were carried on the sides. There were two sizes of letter in use on the small wagons, two-plank high and three-plank high. The big wagons all had two-plank high letters and these were white like the small ones, but were shaded black to the right. On the bottom left hand corner appeared the fleet number and on the bottom right hand corner the letters 'C M R'. All wagons had black ironwork. There was also a clip for carrying a paper ticket giving the bill of lading for each load of coal.

The lettering was painted out during the mine ownership machinations in the 1920s, but some wagons were painted 'Maisel Petroleum Trust' just before the colliery closed finally.

C & M L R Crest

The railway company crest was carried on the side tanks of the two 0–6–2 tank engines. It consisted of the Campbeltown coat of arms slightly modified, surmounted by a North British Railway 4–4–0, and surrounded by the name of the company in full on a white ring. The coat of arms is based on the shields of various branches of the Argyll family. It consists of a quartered shield: on the top left hand corner there is a gold three-towered castle on a green ground. Below it is the Lorne Galley in brown on a silver background. The top right hand corner is quartered and each quarter divided by diagonal lines and the segments are coloured gold and black alternately. The last corner has a black saltire cross and black diamond on a silver ground.

CHAPTER EIGHT

Dreams of Greatness

Now that the Campbeltown and Machrihanish Light Railway has come and gone, it is interesting to consider schemes which were proposed to extend the line and to build up a railway network in Argyllshire. The construction of these lines would certainly have done much to open up a countryside which until well into the twentieth century depended on the sea for transport.

With equal certainty, mechanical road transport would have destroyed any lines so built long before they could have repaid any capital invested in them.

NORTH BRITISH RAILWAY PROPOSALS

The first scheme was the West Highland Railway (Loch Fyne Light Railway) Order of 1898. This provided for a branch from Arrochar on the West Highland Railway to St Catherines on Loch Fyne where directly across the loch is situated Inveraray, seat of the Duke of Argyll. The railway was to be standard gauge and would have left the W H R at Arrochar station and curved round behind Arrochar village to the head of Loch Long. Here a high embankment or viaduct would have been required to take the railway across Glen Loin and along the lower slopes of Ben Arthur (the Cobbler). About three miles from Arrochar the line would have turned north-west up Glen Croe to the Rest and Be Thankful and on down Glen Kinglas to Loch Fyne. On reaching the loch the railway would be high on the hillside and would have inclined down to St Catherines four miles further to the south-west. Here a jetty was to have been built on which the track would terminate

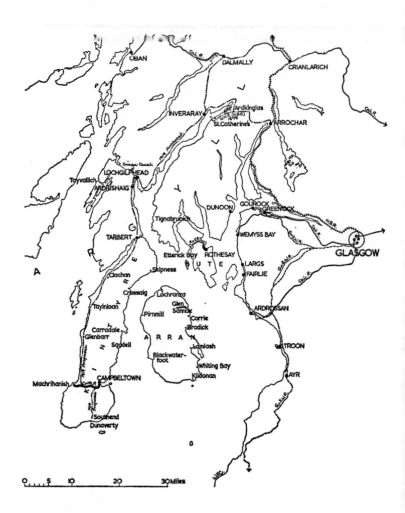

PROPOSALS FOR AN EXTENDED
ARGYLLSHIRE LIGHT RAILWAY SYSTEM 1919.

with facilities for loading and unloading coasters plying in Loch Fyne.

The railway was to be built as a light railway and it was not required to be fenced so long as the engines carried cow-catchers at either end, or at least at one end if turning facilities were provided. Limited signalling was to be provided at passing loops.

This railway was never built but had it been so it must surely have rivalled the other west of Scotland railways for scenic grandeur.

Back in the south, the Campbeltown & Machrihanish had no sooner got off the ground than a line was being proposed from Campbeltown to Southend through the Conie Glen. In August 1907 another line was being proposed from Campbel-town up the west side of Kintyre to Tayinloan where a new quay was to be built to serve the Gigha ferry.

GLASGOW & SOUTH WESTERN RAILWAY PROPOSALS

As the first decade drew to a close, another of the big com-panies cast its eye on Kintyre, this time the Glasgow & South Western Railway. This company enjoyed a virtual monopoly of traffic in Ayrshire and Galloway but was prevented by the natural boundary of the Clyde from pushing northward and westward into the Highlands. The railway owned a fine fleet of paddle steamers and fought the Caledonian Steam Packet Co and to a lesser extent the North British Railway Co for traffic on the Firth of Clyde. There were Caley and Sou'west lines along the south shore of the Clyde and the connecting steamers raced for Dunoon daily. The Caley reached down the Firth to Wemyss Bay and the Sou'west came up from the south to Fairlie and Largs to compete for Rothesay and both com-panies had lines to Ardrossan from whence they sailed successively bigger and faster steamers to Arran.

But Kintyre escaped the railway companies' steamers to a great extent. Macbrayne's *Columba* sailed to Tarbert and, as Macbrayne owned the pier, other companies' steamers hadn't a look in. Campbeltown had its own steamers and both these and the turbines sailed direct from Bridge Wharf, Glasgow.

TARBERT

Skipness

B U T E

Clachan

Lochranza

Cour
Bay

Tayinloan

Pirnmill

Carradale
Glenbarr

A R R A N

Machrihanish

CAMPBELTOWN

Southend

0   5   10   20   30 Miles

GLASGOW & SOUTH WESTERN
RAILWAY PROPOSALS circa 1910.

The Glasgow & South Western steamers were allowed to
ply to Campbeltown but only on an excursion basis. Regular
services were forbidden to them. However, in 1901, the G & S W
was advertising a sailing in conjunction with the Williamson-
Buchanan steamer *Strathmore* from Fairlie to the north-west
Arran piers and Carradale. The possibility of tapping the
Kintyre traffic somewhere between Tarbert and Campbeltown
was good, provided a transport system was there to handle
the shore side of things. The two available piers, one at Skipness
and one at Carradale had little adjacent traffic. The Sou'west
decided to organise Kintyre. Two railways were proposed.

The northern line was to start at Skipness pier and follow
the shore south westwards for two miles and then turn inland
up Glenrisdell and curve round to the clachan of Clachan at
the mouth of West Loch Tarbert. Here a pier would be built

in Ronachan Bay which could serve the islands of Isla and Jura in competition with Macbraynes.

The second railway was to be much more ambitious and was shown to be not physically connected with the first and may have been an alternative or later proposal. This railway would have commenced at a new pier in Cour Bay and again followed the shore for two miles before turning inland alongside the Sunadale and Narachan Burn to the west coast at Tayinloan where the ferry to the island of Gigha is situated. The route then turned south and ran down the coastal shelf to Drumlemble where it crossed the existing C & M L R. A connection swung round to join the C & M and allow trains to run into Campbeltown. The main line carried on down the centre of the Mull of Kintyre in the Conie Glen to Southend where a pier at Dunaverty was considered for possible sailings to Ireland. A new hotel was proposed at Ballochantuy and a new golf course at Killean, both to be owned by the railway.

The G & S W intended taking over the C & M L R and using its right of way into Campbeltown. It would therefore have been in a position to run coal and other exports either to Southend for shipment to Ireland or to Cour Bay for shipment to Glasgow.

The railway was to have been narrow gauge and 3 ft 0 in and 2 ft 6 in were mentioned but possibly the existence of the C & M L R would have resulted in 2 ft 3 in being adopted. For its main line, bigger Barclay tanks of either 4–6–0 or 2–6–4 wheel arrangement were suggested.

The G & S W however had second thoughts on the matter and denied enthusiasts the sight of *Argyll* and *Atlantic* in Sou'west green.

After the Great War had finished and men started to look to ways of making the country a place fit for heroes to live in, there was a great upsurge in interest in light railways. The success of the War Department's light railways in France for serving the front lines and the obvious advantages of rail over the then road transport prompted many people to believe that here was a solution to the development of rural areas where full scale railways were not justified either for capital cost or for traffic expected. The Belgium Societé Nationale des Chemins de Fer Vicinaux (SNCV) was held up as a shining example of a complete narrow gauge network complementary to the national railway system.

The Rural Transport (Scotland) Committee was formed and in 1919 it published its report. Proposals had been put before it for the construction of a light railway from Campbeltown to Tarbert and of a branch off the Campbeltown & Machrihanish Light Railway to serve the Southend district. The district committee did not, however, appear to consider that they would be justified in pressing these proposals and the transport committee concluded that the existing requirements of the district could be met by road-borne traffic.

In this district they were much interested in the working of the C & M L R, the only independent narrow gauge line in Scotland. The transport committee noted that for its revenue it had depended to a large extent on passenger traffic (mainly summer excursion traffic from Greenock and Wemyss Bay) and on the conveyance of coal from the colliery near Machrihanish. It might have been expected that in a good farming district such as this the conveyance of agricultural requirements and produce to and from the farms would have formed a substantial amount of traffic of the line but the committee found that it was practically nil. This was attributed by the directors to the short length of the railway (six miles) and to the fact that farmers using the line had to cart between the railway and their farms and again between the railway terminus at Campbeltown and the general steamboat quay, and consequently preferred to cart the whole distance from the farm to the ship's side and incidentally save the extra handling of goods. The committee considered this as constituting an argument in favour of the use of road motor transport for the conveyance of goods in rural districts where the average distance of farms from an existing railway or steamer service is comparatively short. The committee recommended that as the terminus of the railway at Campbeltown was near the general steamboat quay and in order to obtain the full usefulness of the railway for general traffic purposes, it would be necessary to lay a railway siding connection on the quay. This could be done at small expense.

ARGYLLSHIRE RAILWAY PROPOSALS

At the same time that the committee were so pessimistic about rail transport, schemes were being discussed in Kintyre for an even more ambitious project, that of a railway being built to join either the Caledonian at Dalmally or the North British at Arrochar. Should this have ever been built it would probably have been *the* most uneconomic railway development in these islands. J. R. Moreton Macdonald of Largie was sufficiently keen on the Campbeltown to Tarbert section to offer the six mile route through his estates free of charge and also to subscribe to any company that would be formed. He considered that a circular tour formed of Macbraynes' sailing to Tarbert by *Columba*, a railway trip down the west coast of Kintyre to Campbeltown and thence back by *Queen Alexandra* would be a financial success. Other parties bemoaned the fact that farmers often had to cart their produce up to ten or even twenty miles to a port for shipment and this sorely tried their resources. P. Jeffrey Mackie of Glenreasdell followed up Largie's offer with his own of ten miles right of way and opined that plenty of rails would be available from the government surplus sales in France.

The first proposal for a line north of Tarbert was to connect with the Caledonian Railway at Dalmally, the route being along the west shore of Loch Fyne to Inveraray and thence cutting inland through Glen Aray to Loch Awe. A short run up the eastern shore of Loch Awe would effect a connection with the existing railway. No sooner was this idea put forward than the West Highland Railway's proposal of 1898 was cited and the proposals changed to provide a railway to Arrochar instead. By now, of course, narrow gauge was being considered but the advantages of the smaller formation were slightly reduced by the proposal to tunnel through the Rest and Be Thankful pass from Glen Kinglas to Glen Croe, about one and a half miles! Even in 1919 it was considered impossible to build a road suitable for other than horse-drawn traffic over this route. Yet another proposal was for a rack railway on the Abt system to negotiate the Rest and Be Thankful. However sanity prevailed in the end and posterity was never able to 'enjoy' the eighty mile journey behind a government surplus Baldwin 4–6–0 tank. It is significant however that it was only after the 1939-45 war that a new road was opened over the Rest and Be Thankful. The old road remains, and is still used for hill-climbing trials.

Appendixes

1 Drawings of rolling stock

2 Other railways

3 Spares supplied for locomotives

4 Geological features of Machrihanish coalfield

5 Company business

6 Railway verse

O·4·OST/O·4·2ST locomotive 'CHEVALIER'.

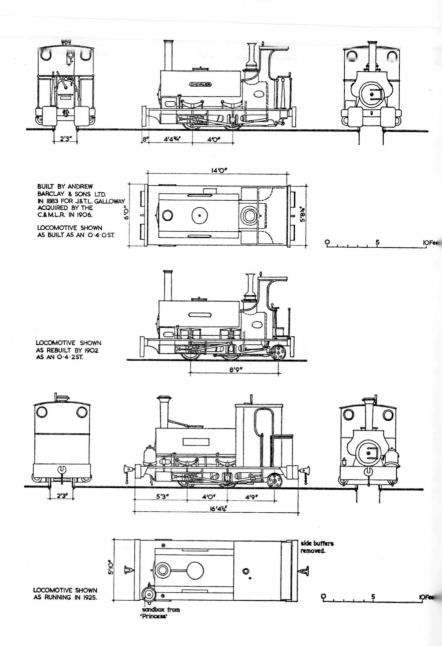

BUILT BY ANDREW
BARCLAY & SONS LTD.
IN 1883 FOR J.&T.L. GALLOWAY.
ACQUIRED BY THE
C.&M.L.R. IN 1906.

LOCOMOTIVE SHOWN
AS BUILT AS AN O·4·OST.

LOCOMOTIVE SHOWN
AS REBUILT BY 1902
AS AN O·4·2ST.

LOCOMOTIVE SHOWN
AS RUNNING IN 1925.

sandbox from
'Princess'

side buffers
removed.

0·4·2 T locomotive 'PRINCESS'.

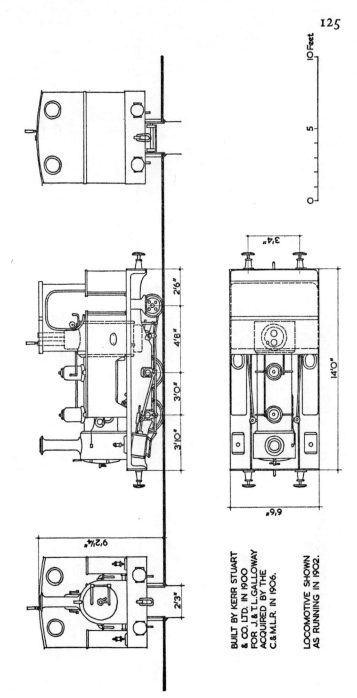

BUILT BY KERR STUART
& CO. LTD. IN 1900
FOR J.&T.L.GALLOWAY
ACQUIRED BY THE
C.&M.L.R. IN 1906.

LOCOMOTIVE SHOWN
AS RUNNING IN 1902.

10 Feet

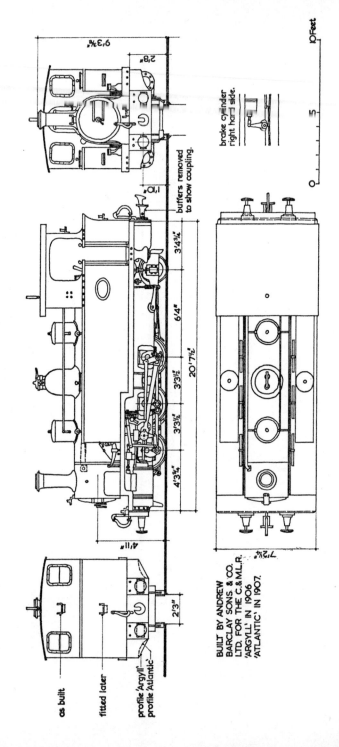

O·6·2T locomotives 'ARGYLL' & 'ATLANTIC'

9'3¾"

2'8"

1'10"

buffers removed
to show coupling.

3'4¾"

6'4"

20'7½"

3'3½"

3'3½"

4'3¾"

4'11"

2'3"

as built

fitted later

profile 'Argyll'
profile 'Atlantic'

brake cylinder
right hand side.

7'2½"

BUILT BY ANDREW
BARCLAY SONS & CO.
LTD. FOR THE C.& M.L.R.
'ARGYLL' IN 1906
'ATLANTIC' IN 1907.

10 Feet
5
0

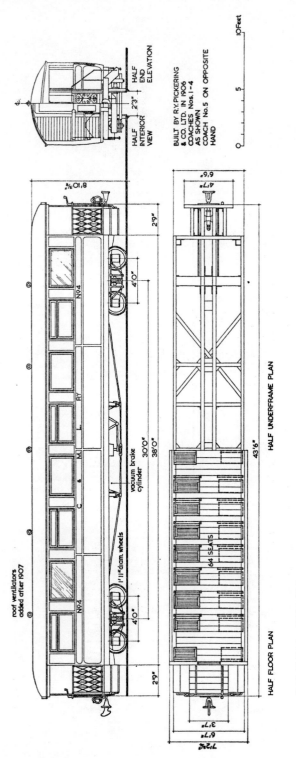

HALF END ELEVATION

HALF INTERIOR VIEW

2'3"

BUILT BY R.Y. PICKERING
& CO. LTD. IN 1906
COACHES Nos. 1-4
AS SHOWN
COACH No. 5 ON OPPOSITE
HAND

10 Feet

5

0

8'10½"

2'9"

No. 4

4'0"

C & M. L. RY

30'0"

38'0"

vacuum brake
cylinder

1'11" diam. wheels

4'0"

2'9"

No. 4

roof ventilators
added after 1907

HALF UNDERFRAME PLAN

9'6"

4'7"

43'6"

64 SEATS

HALF FLOOR PLAN

3'7"

6'7"

7'2½"

SALOON COACH

127

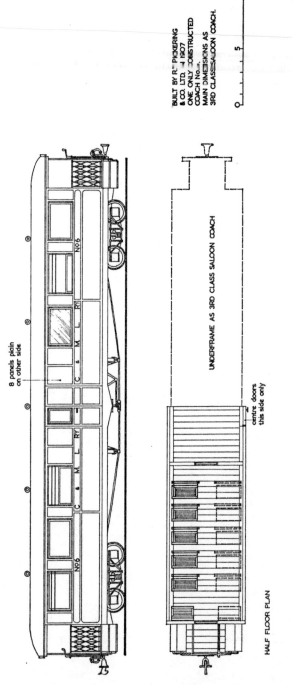

8 panels plain
on other side

No6 C & M L RY C & M L RY No6

HALF FLOOR PLAN

centre doors
this side only

UNDERFRAME AS 3RD CLASS SALOON COACH

BUILT BY Rᵀ PICKERING
& CO. LTD. — 1907
ONE ONLY CONSTRUCTED
COACH No. .
MAIN DIMENSIONS AS
3RD CLASS SALOON COACH.

0   5   10 Feet

SALOON BRAKE

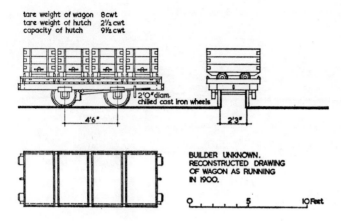

tare weight of wagon 8 cwt
tare weight of hutch 2½ cwt
capacity of hutch 9½ cwt

2'0" diam.
chilled cast iron wheels

4'6"

2'3"

BUILDER UNKNOWN.
RECONSTRUCTED DRAWING
OF WAGON AS RUNNING
IN 1900.

0   5   10 Feet

Colliery hutch carrier
built for the Campbeltown Coal Co.

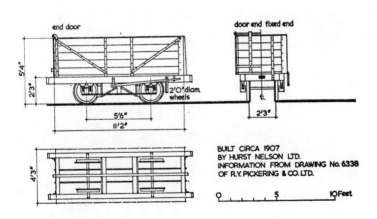

end door

door end fixed end

5'4"

2'3"

2'0" diam.
wheels

5'6"

11'2"

2'3"

4'3"

BUILT CIRCA 1907
BY HURST NELSON LTD.
INFORMATION FROM DRAWING No. 6338
OF R.Y. PICKERING & CO. LTD.

0   5   10 Feet

3¼ ton coal wagon
built for the Campbeltown Coal Co.

H

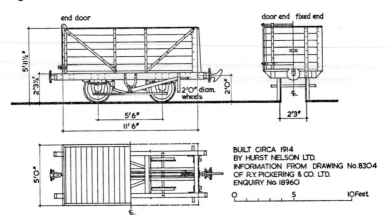

BUILT CIRCA 1914
BY HURST NELSON LTD.
INFORMATION FROM DRAWING No. 8304
OF R.Y. PICKERING & CO. LTD.
ENQUIRY No. 18960

4½ ton coal wagon
built for the Campbeltown Coal Co.

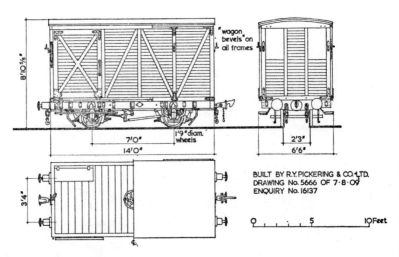

BUILT BY R.Y. PICKERING & CO. LTD.
DRAWING No. 5666 OF 7·8·09
ENQUIRY No. 16137

7 ton goods brake van
built for the C. & M.L.R.

SSENGER STOCK PROPOSED BUT NOT BUILT.

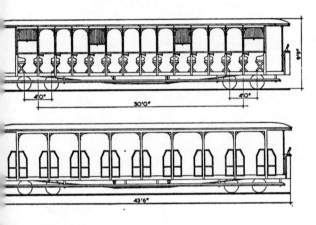

9'0"

4'0"   30'0"   4'0"

43'6"

PEN CARRIAGES

0   5   10 Feet

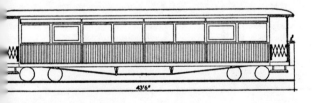

43'6"

D CLASS SALOON

PROPOSED BY
R.Y. PICKERING & CO. LTD.
IN THEIR DRAWING No 3206
DATED 5·12·04.

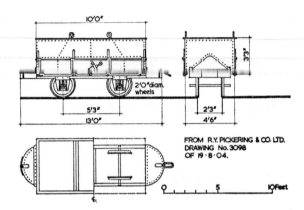

Proposed hopper coal wagon
for the Campbeltown Coal Co.

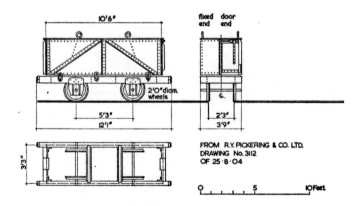

Proposed coal wagon with detachable body
for the Campbeltown Coal Co.

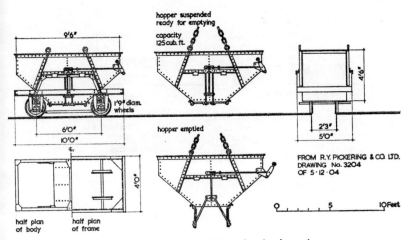

hopper suspended
ready for emptying
capacity
125 cub. ft.

hopper emptied

9'6"

1'9" diam.
wheels

6'0"
10'0"

half plan
of body

half plan
of frame

4'0"

4'6"

2'3"
5'0"

FROM R.Y. PICKERING & CO. LTD.
DRAWING No. 3204
OF 5·12·04

0 ____ 5 ____ 10 Feet

Proposed hopper coal wagon with self closing doors
for the C.&M.L.R.

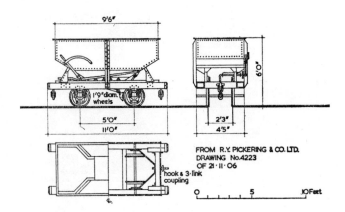

9'6"

1'9" diam.
wheels

5'0"
11'0"

6'0"

2'3"
4'5"

hook & 3·link
coupling

FROM R.Y. PICKERING & CO. LTD.
DRAWING No. 4223
OF 21·11·06

0 ____ 5 ____ 10 Feet

Proposed 3½ ton hopper coal wagon
for use on the C.&M.L.R.

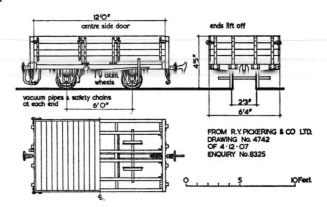

Proposed 5 ton open goods wagon
for the C.& M.L.R.

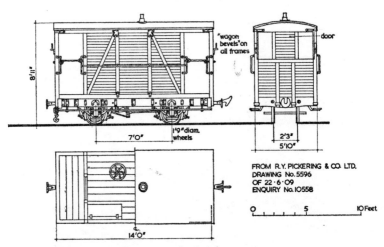

Proposed 7 ton goods brake van
for the C.& M.L.R.

OTHER RAILWAYS IN THE AREA

THE ARDKINGLAS RAILWAY

The Campbeltown & Machrihanish Light Railway was not the first narrow gauge railway in Argyllshire. Away up at the top of Loch Fyne lies the estate of Ardkinglas. It is situated at the western end of the road through Glen Kinglas from the Rest an' be Thankful pass. The road turns north round the top of Loch Fyne and south to Strachur. Each road slants steeply down to sea level forming a triangle of which the west side is Loch Fyne. Along this side of the loch, there was built in the middle of the nineteenth century, a 2 ft narrow gauge railway. This railway was partly to provide transport in the estate and partly as a garden toy for the then proprietor. Rolling stock consisted of a steam locomotive, an open passenger carriage, and some wagons. The layout was quite extensive and facilities included a small engine shed with a service pit (still traceable), a station and a tunnel. The station was blown down the same night as the first Tay Bridge but unlike the latter was not replaced. The northern terminus of the line was alongside a boat house on an artificial loch made in the shape of the Caspian Sea and still called the Caspian. A pier was built out into this loch to serve a small paddle steamer and miniature naval battles are reputed to have been staged there. To this day, there stands in the trees near the Caspian a two-storey 'Wendy' house where the ceilings are a mere 4 ft high and only children can stand upright.

About the same time as the Campbeltown & Machrihanish Railway was being formed in the early 1900s, the Ardkinglas railway was dismantled and the equipment sold off. The locomotive and rails went for scrap and finished up at Tayvallich on Loch Sween. As late as 1951 the boiler of the engine was lying on the beach at Tayvallich. A photograph of this boiler was published in the *Scottish Field* of September 1952 and the author of the accompanying article claimed that the oscillating engines of the Caspian's paddle steamer could be found in the undergrowth behind Taynich Old Mill near Tayvallich.

Though not a part of Argyllshire, the island of Arran lies adjacent to the east side of the Kintyre peninsula. On the northeast side of Arran there was a narrow gauge railway built up Glen Sannox to a barytes mine. The main line of this railway consisted of a long balanced incline worked by gravity. Halfway up there was a passing loop. Below the passing loop where there could only be one end of the cable at the one time, there was single track. Above the passing loop, to avoid the cables getting fouled in pointwork, there was a three-rail formation where the middle rail was common to trucks running on either outer rail. At the top of the incline were lines going off into various adits and some lesser inclines. At the foot of the main incline the track split into four and ran out on the level over two large concrete hoppers. From the underside of these, two tracks emerged to cross the main Brodick to Lochranza road on the level. The lines joined immediately and then crossed the river Sannox on a timber trestle bridge. Between here and the shore, the ground was level but the railway was carried on a low embankment and out on to a timber pier for loading small ships. This pier was not of normal Clyde construction but consisted mainly of unhewn logs and trestles. Haulage on the lower line was by horse or manpower. The wagons used on the upper railway were quite small wooden affairs but those on the lower stretch were well-built railway wagons carrying about two tons.

The Sannox Railway was used during the first thirty years of the twentieth century but had fallen into disuse before the second world war broke out.

APPENDIX 3

SPARES SUPPLIED FOR LOCOMOTIVES

Kerr Stuart No 717 *Princess*

Date	Order No	Items
3/ 1/01	9105	1 pair Rocking Shafts & Brackets
23/ 1/02	2495	2 Leading & 2 Driving Springs
10/ 2/02	2591	1 Set Brake Blocks

Date	Order No	Items
9/ 6/02	3091	4 Springs for Leading & Driving Wheels
		1 Set ditto for each piston
		1 Spring for Bogie Wheel
	3092	2 Bogie Axle Boxes & Brasses
3/ 6/02	3149	4 Spring Buffers
21/10/02	3555	2 Sets Brake Blocks, 2 Fusible Plugs,
		2 Quadrant Die Blocks
11/ 2/03	3997	1 Bogie Spring
27/ 4/03	4226-7	2 Sets each Large & Small end Conn Rod Brasses
	4328	4 Sets Coupling Rod Brasses
	4329-30	1 Front Cylinder Cover, 2 Exhaust Pipes
	4340	4 Main & 2 Bogie Axle Box Brasses
25/ 6/03	4425	2 Sets Brake Blocks
30/ 7/03	4617	1 Pair Bogie Wheels & Axle
	4618	4 Springs for Leading & Driving Wheels
		1 Spring for Bogie
		1 Set Piston Rings
9/11/03	4925	1 Complete set of Springs
16/12/03	5057	1 Set Axle Boxes & Brasses for Pony Trucks
6/ 4/04	5426	2 Steam Valves for Injector
22/ 4/04	5483	1 Set Axle Boxes & Brasses
13/ 5/04	5591	1 Set Brake Blocks
4/11/04	6155	1 Set Brake Blocks
24/11/04	6205	1 Bogie Spring
7/ 3/05	6548	1 Set Main Axle Box Guides
29/ 9/05	7118	1 Piston Rod
18/12/05	7332	1 Set Brasses for Pony Wheels
		1 „ „ for Coupling & Conn Rods
		1 „ „ for Crossheads
		1 C I Bend Steam Pipe
8/ 1/06	7389	2 Axle Boxes complete with Brasses
1/ 5/06	7758	1 Eccentric Hoop
20/ 8/06	7970	2 Check Valves
8/ 9/06	8020	12 Boiler Tubes
8/11/06	8166	1 Set of Driving & Coupled Wheel Axle Boxes
26/ 4/07	8605	1 Brass for Coupling Rod Ends of Leading Wheels
15/11/07	9185	1 Complete Brass for Coupling Rod End
		1 „ „ for Crank Pin of Driving Wheels

Date	Order No	Items
3/ 2/08	9432	2 Fusible Plugs
28/ 3/08	9628	2 Fusible Plugs
1/ 4/08	9638	1 Steam Regulator Valve
	9639	2 Main Bearing Springs
	9640	1 Bogie Bearing Spring
20/ 8/10	5006	1 Bogie Spring
23/ 1/10	5478	1 Steam Valve for Injector
		1 Spare Spindle for ditto
16/ 1/13	8920	1 Exhaust Pipe
21/ 5/13	9534	2 Bearing Springs, 9 Plates

A B S & Co No 1049 *Argyll*

Description of Part	Date
Repair Springs	27/ 4/16
Ferrules	17/12/16
Coupling Rod Bushes	25/ 5/17
Coupling & Connecting Rod Bushes, Crosshead Slipper	16/ 1/18
Bearing Springs	20/ 8/19
Crown Stay Bolts	6/ 2/20
Quadrant Brackets	11/ 2/20
Spring Links & Brackets	18/ 2/20
Firebars	5/ 5/20
Springs	29/ 6/20
Blow-Off Cock	18/ 8/20
Firebars	21/ 3/21
Firebars	29/ 6/21
Coupling Rod & Flycrank Bushes	21/ 2/22
Crown Stay Bolt Nuts	13/ 3/22
Spring Links	5/ 3/22
Bogie Spring	20/ 9/22
$\frac{5}{8}$" Water Gauge Cocks	3/ 2/23
Pillar Spring Guides	9/ 3/23
Bogie A B Bushes	26/ 4/23
Crosshead Slippers	8/ 6/23
Valve Spindle	11/ 8/23
Driving Spring & Bogie Spring	28/ 8/23
Coupling & Connecting Rod Bushes	23/10/23
S Box Barrel & S Box Door complete	23/10/23
Firebars	29/10/23

Description of Part	Date
Stay Bars	30/10/23
Blower Studs	28/ 1/24
Spring Pillar Guides	5/ 2/24
Mud Plugs	9/ 2/24
Springs	9/ 2/24
Rev Shaft & Bushes	27/ 2/24
Rev Handle Bracket	27/ 2/24
Brake Hangers	13/ 3/24
Brake Blocks & Brackets	13/ 3/24
Brake Rods	13/ 3/24
Lifting Lever & Bracket	21/ 3/24
Valve Guide Bracket Liners	3/ 9/24
Brake Blocks & Piston Rings	10/12/24
Firebars	11/12/24
Boiler	31/1/25
Exhaust Nozzle	10/ 3/25
Bogie Coupling Pin	11/ 3/25
Injector Cones & Tee Stand Spindle	10/ 3/25
Quadrant Blocks & Asbestos Wadding	14/ 3/25
Brake Blocks	8/ 9/25
Fusible Plug	9/ 9/25
Bogie Spring Links, Knuckle Washers, Spring Links & Rocker Pins	29/10/25
Re-Tyre Wheels for Bogie, Bogie Tyres	22/ 2/26
Brake Blocks, Bogie Springs	21/ 6/26
S Box Piston Rings	24/ 9/26
Fusible Plug	17/ 3/27
Brake Blocks	18/ 3/27
Ferrules, Tubes	18/ 7/27
Coup. Beams & Bkts. Coup. Rod Bushes & Coup. Rod Pin and Crosshead Slippers, List of Material	1/ 2/28
Coupling Rod Bushes	9/ 3/28
Coupling Rod Pins	2/ 4/28
Coupling Rod Steel Bushes	5/ 4/28
Bar Stays	12/ 4/28
Bogie Springs	13/ 6/28
Fusible Plugs	23/10/28
Spring Links & Pins	22/ 1/29
Turn-up Tyres, Axle Box Bushes	28/ 3/29
Drain Cocks RH	2/ 4/29
Fusible Plugs	25/10/29
Brake Blocks	1/11/29

Description of Part	Date
Bogie Springs	1/ 7/30
Spring Gear Pins & Collars	16/ 1/30

A B S & Co No 1098 *Atlantic*

Description of Part	Date
Springs	15/ 9/16
Piston Rings	4/ 5/17
Exhaust Nozzle	17/ 5/17
Crosshead Slipper	22/ 3/18
Tyres	1/ 4/18
Crosshead Slippers	19/ 9/18
Springs & Plates for Spongebox	15/10/18
A B Bushes	17/10/18
Bogie Springs	23/ 1/19
Springs	4/ 4/19
Quadrant Brackets	11/ 2/20
Water Gauge Cock, L H	30/ 7/20
Copper Stays & Instructions	17/12/20
Blower Valve	25/ 1/21
Bushes for Coup. Rod & Flycrank Rod; P R Neck Rings, Brake Blocks, Coup. & Connecting Rod Bolts & Nuts	21/12/21
Spring Links	5/ 4/22
Bogie Springs	20/ 9/22
⅝″ Water Gauge Cocks	3/ 2/23
Crosshead Slippers	5/ 2/23
Pressure Gauge Cock	8/ 2/23
Driving Springs, Bogie Springs	28/ 8/23
Blower Studs	28/ 1/24
Rev Shaft & Bushes, Rev Handle Bracket	27/ 2/24
Drain Cocks	23/ 5/24
Piston Rings	10/12/24
Firebricks	27/ 1/25
Springs for Bogie	2/ 6/25
Bogie Coupling Pin	11/3/25
Bogie Coupling Pin	2/ 4/25
Firehole Protectors	9/ 4/25
Deflector Plates	10/ 4/25
Brake Screw & Link	14/ 4/25
Brake Gear, Brake Blocks	13/ 5/25
Connecting Rod Wedges & Bolts	15/10/25
Spring Links & Knuckle Washers (Bogie)	29/10/25

Description of Part	Date
Spring Links & Rocker Pins	29/10/25
Firebox, Direct Stays	7/ 1/26
Tyres, Boiler Repairs	6/ 1/26
Firebrick Studs & Deflector Plate	20-25/ 1/26
Bogie Springs, Brake Blocks	21/ 6/26
Spring Brackets & Beams	3/ 2/26
Foundation Ring	6/ 2/26
Boiler Repairs	5/ 2/26
S Box Door & Mountings	1/ 3/26
S Box Piston Rings	24/ 9/26
Fusible Plug	27/ 3/27
Connecting Rod Wedge & Bolts	12/ 7/27
Spring Compensating Beam & Pins	27/ 9/27
Adjusting Screws and Blocks, Brake Blocks	20/ 1/28
Crankpin Nuts	21/ 1/28
Coupling & Connecting Rod Bushes	26/ 1/28
Bogie Springs	13/ 6/28
Spring Links & Pins	22/ 1/29
L H Valve Spindle	3/ 4/29
Fusible Plugs	25/10/29
Brake Blocks	1/11/29
Bogie Springs	1/ 7/30

APPENDIX 4

GEOLOGICAL FEATURES

OF

MACHRIHANISH COALFIELD

The Machrihanish Coalfield is situated on the west side of the Kintyre Peninsula, a few miles from Campbeltown, and occupies a low lying tract of country almost completely covered by superficial materials—raised beach deposits, recent alluvion and sand dunes. Exposures of sedimentary rocks are limited to the interrupted series of shore reefs accessible only at low tides. Accordingly, practically all the information regarding the succession and structure within the coalfield is derived from boring and mining operations. The general succession of carboniferous rocks so far established is as follows:—

Productive Coal Measures .... about 530 feet
Millstone grit (mainly volcanic rocks) .... about 485 feet
Upper Limestone Group .... about 290 feet
Limestone Coal Group ,,,,,,,,,,,,,,,,,,,,,,,,,,,,,,,, about 390 feet
Lateritic clays and volcanic detritus of variable thickness resting
on weathered lavas.

No 2 West Parkfergus Bore in 1948 gave the following section:—

Coal	2 ft	4 in	at	15	fathoms
Coal		8 in	at	21	fathoms
Coal	5 ft	9 in	at	30	fathoms
Coal		11 in	at	35	fathoms
Coal	1 ft	10 in	at	40	fathoms
Coal		2 in	at	45	fathoms
Coal	1 ft	0 in	at	56	fathoms
Cannel		8 in	at	63	fathoms
Coal	1 ft	7 in	at	64	fathoms
Coal		9 in	at	74	fathoms
Coal		7 in	at	81	fathoms

The mining in Argyll Colliery has been in the Limestone Coal
Group and the series is as follows:—

Index Limestone		—	
Strata	42 ft	0 in	
Cannel	2 ft	10 in	
Strata	72 ft	0 in	
Kilkivan Coal	4 ft	6 in to 7 ft	
Strata	24 ft	0 in	
Sandstone	82 ft	0 in	
Blaes	2 ft	0 in	
Main Coal	12 ft	0 in	
Strata	2 ft	0 in	
Underfoot Coal	4 ft	0 in	

From the foregoing notes it is evident that the quality of the
coal in the Machrihanish coalfield has always been the main draw-
back. The coal is suitable for commercial use in boilers designed
for its use, but the remoteness of the field from the industrial belt
of Scotland raises a transport problem which is unsurmountable.
Domestically the coal gives a good heat but leaves a large quantity
of white ash.

APPENDIX 5

COMPANY BUSINESS

TYPICAL ANNUAL STATEMENTS

	1913	1919
Gross Receipts	£2,906–19– 4	£4,792–12–11
Expenses	2,305–15– 4	4,102–12– 2
Net Profit	601– 4– 0	690– 0– 9
Interest on Deb.	300– 0– 0	300– 0– 0
Rent	159– 0– 0	124– 0– 0
C/F	142– 4– 0	266– 0– 9
	601– 4– 0	690– 0– 9

Bal B/F	£126	£ 70
	+ 142	+ 266
Bal C/F	£268– 0– 0	£336– 0– 0

TRAFFIC RECEIPTS

	1913	1919
Passenger	£1,947	£3,476
Freight	920	1,280
Misc.	40	37

TRAFFIC CARRIED

		1913	1919	1923	1924
Passenger	ordinary	79,887	86,678	76,054	80,197
	workmen	27,125	25,000	8,712	9,234
	+ 1 & 7/10th season ticket				
Freight (tons)		431	281	600	300
Coal (tons)		29,591	47,727	21,373	21,578
Engine Mileage	passenger			14,790	14,654
	goods			2,609	2,655

1919

Superintendent's expenses			25
Permanent Way			888
Rolling Stock	locos	181	
	carriages	32	213
			———
			£1,126

Loco running:

	Wages	518
	Fuel	824
	Other	229
		———
		£1,571

Traffic Salaries and Wages	386
Other	129
General Charges	139
	———
	£654

PROFITABILITY
OF
C & M L R

Year	Dividend	Reserve	C/F
1906– 7	2½%	£250	
1907– 8	2 %	—	
1908– 9	—	£250	
1909–10	—	£500	
1910–11	—	—	
1911–12	2 %	—	
1912–13	2 %	£200	£229

For the next period of five months from August to 31 December
1913, the net income after paying fixed charges and bringing
forward balance from 1912-13 was £268 which was carried
forward to 1914. No dividend was paid after 1913.

APPENDIX 6

RAILWAY AND CANAL VERSE

THE OLD DRUMLEMBLE CANAL

'Leaves *but* a wrack behind'.

(from the *Argyllshire Herald* of 21 August 1880)

One glibly descants on the beauty of streams,
    Or the floods that from precipice fall;
Another on torrents in ecstasy dreams—
    My subject's the ancient canal.

My fancy e'en yet awakes with delight
    As memory its windings review;
'Mid the scenes of the past it lies smiling and bright,
    And its banks with fresh verdure renews.

By its hoof-trodden brink, with satchel in hand,
    I saunter'd or skipped to the school;
But, truth to confess, too long I would stand
    To scan the contents of the pool.

Let tropical regions their produce display,
    And botanists dote on their forms;
Let palms and bananas the tourist repay
    For his travels in quest of their charms:

The pliant, slim sedges that bow'd to the wind—
    Created, I fancied, for boys—
Had virtues more precious—at least to my mind—
    And wakened much livelier joys.

From their supple materials moulded with skill
    A tiny flotilla I launch'd on the wave,
I doubt if such rapture Lord Nelson did fill
    As he marshall'd his fleet and admonish'd the brave.

I

True type of the crocodile cleaving the Nile,
  'Mid lilies and bullrushes tall,
Small lizards and asps would your leisure beguile
  By the brink of the ancient canal.

The crazy old gaabert sail'd slowly along
  With her cargo of timber or coal;
What volumes of blessings(!) left many a tongue
  At her sluggish approach to the goal.

The slower the better for truants like *me*—
  How nimbly I sprang from the bank,
And leapt on her beams with boisterous glee,
  While the pilot got fierce at my prank!

Kind pilot; though oft a bit coal he would raise,
  When Urchins jump'd on in a row
And threatened to punish their impudent ways,
  That coal he never *did* throw.

When I was a laddie officials had *hearts*—
  They might menace with 'Courts' and a jail;
But though we got shakings and troublesome starts,
  The breeze never rose to a gale.

When winter beleaguered the drumly old pool,
  And its surface made firm as a floor,
Then truant and student abandoned the school
  More welcome achievements to score.

From morning till evening—and often beyond—
  Oblivious of books and of care,
Like eagles we sped o'er the crust of the pond,
  To parents' and teachers' despair.

No water more clearly reflected the skies,
  The outline of clouds and their hue;
No glass to my features more truly replies—
  My photo seems hardly so true.

Here gudgeons and perches the angler allured
  From villages, mountains and glens;
With the luck of his rod the fisher secured
  The vigour that exercise lends.

Here friendships for life were cemented in youth,
    And sweetened as seasons revolve;
And though we're apart as the north from the south,
    No space can our union dissolve.

Yet sad were the thought in the emigrant's breast
    Were he now to revisit the lake
Where in summer he'd wade to the wren's tiny nest,
    Or the duck from its slumbering wake.

The waters have fled like the mist of the morn,
    Deserting their time-honoured bed;
No longer their windings the landscape adorn,
    Nor moisture o'er neighbourhood shed.

Like a spirit unbound, what was flowing and free
    Has pass'd from its motionless 'coil';
Now it sparkles on roses or rolls to the sea,
    And now it refreshes the soil.

But the channel is buried in rubbish and reeds—
    At once its own carcase and grave—
The refuge of adders and vagrant seeds,
    Unsightly to saint and to knave.

Yet, though now repulsive thy trenches appear,
    Thy graces I fondly recall;
To my bosom thy features will ever be dear,
    Smooth, tortuous, placid canal.

ON THE OPENING OF THE 'KINTYRE RAILWAY'

(from Machrihanish SWRI Village History Book 1966)

    Like voices of springtime to the glen
        Like summer to the vale,
    So is the news to Campbeltown
        That I'm just gaun to tell;
    For gloomy winter bleak and cold,
        Nae mair we'll need tae fear,
    We'll get our fuel cheap and good
        Brought by the 'Pioneer'.

Hark! there she's comin' doon the brae,
  Along by Crossel Hill,
A train o' waggons close behind—
  I hear the whistle shrill.
Go spread the news through a' the toon
  Wi' joy the news they'll hear;
Oor hielan' line is open noo—
  There comes the 'Pioneer'.

Her coals will bless the poorest hame,
  And cheer the humblest hearth,
Although in other parts they're dear,
  No more we'll dread their dearth.
The coals that come frae other lands
  Let them be cheap or dear,
We'll rather hae oor hielan' coals
  Brought by the 'Pioneer'.

The Frenchmen, and the Prussian, too,
  Will smile when they are told
As soon's their cargo they discharge
  Wi' coals we'll stow the hold,
And when they reach their native hame,
  And frien's begin to speer
Where did they get their coals, they'll say—
  ''Twas by the "Pioneer".'

The coals that come frae 'Auld Coalhill'
  Are cheap as coals can be,
They're eighteen shillings for a ton,
  When left in at the ree.
'Twill make the Laggan flourish yet
  We'll gie a hearty cheer—
Success attend oor hielan' line,
  God speed the 'Pioneer'.

                              J. McMurchy

THE HIELAN' RAILWAY

(from Machrihanish SWRI Village History Book 1966)

Oh! Have ye heard the news, my frien'?
About this company, I mean
They say they're going to lay a line
And ca't the Hielan' Railway.

Chorus: With locomotive swift and strong
Upon the line we'll dash along,
The people they will quickly throng
To see our Hielan' Railway.

The moorland folk will run wi' fricht,
And hide themselves far oot o' sicht,
Sayin' 'Tougal, run wi' a' your micht,
Auld Nick is on the railway'.

Chorus—

To Belfast trip no more we'll go,
Nor yet to see Ayr cattle show,
For better sport we'll have, you know,
Upon our Hielan' Railway.

Chorus—

Excursions daily you will see
From the Salt Pans unto the Quay,
Then blythe and merry we shall be
When seated on the railway.

Chorus—

The Campbeltonians when they please
May sit and sail in't at their ease,
And only pay a few bawbees
For a hurl upon the railway.

Chorus—

Success unto these gentlemen
Shall echo loud from hill and glen,
For our conductors weel do ken
  How to lay a railway,

J. McMurchy

A RAILWAY O' OOR AIN

(from the *Campbeltown Courier* commemorating
the opening of the Campbeltown & Machrihanish
Light Railway in August, 1906)

Oor toon ye'd hardly ken the noo
It looks sae big an' braw,
Richt prood they'll be tae see it
They that's been a while awa',
For wi' motor cars an' sich like
It's up tae date that's plain
An' noo tae cap it a', we've got a
Railway o' oor ain.

A Railway o' oor ain nae less,
A Railway o' oor ain,
If ye've yer doots jist come and see't,
This Railway o' oor ain.

Jist roon' aboot the auld quay
Heid and stannin' on the line,
Ye'll see some bonnie carriages
A' painted up sae fine,
Noo tak' ye'r sate in ane o' them
An' a' ye'r cares'll vanish,
Afore ye'r far upon the road that
leads to Machrihanish.

An when ye'r on the Railway ance
Ye'll sure be on't again
O' man it's gran' the very thocht
We've a Railway o' oor ain.

When the Railway first was spoken
'O' some folk wad hum an' haw,
An' saw tae ain anither, it wad never
dae at a'
But noo it's an accomplished fac',
As ony ane can see,
They're jist as keen tae tak' their sates
as aither you or me.

An it's Railway this, an' Railway that,
An Railway ower again,
Ye'd think tae hear them blawin' noo
That the Railway was their ain.

Ye often hear o' falk gau'n oot a jaunt
Tae the saut pans,
An' many gather there they say
Frae far off foreign lands,
Then what's tae hinner us at hame
Tae tak' the guid o't tae,
When the Railway runs maist
Frae the door tae Machrihanish Bay.

An' we'll tak' oor freens out wi' us
An' we'll a' go back again,
For it's easy come an' easy go
On this Railway o' oor ain.

An' noo I maun be stoppen', I hae
Kep' ye far ower lang,
Ye see, I got so happy ower the subjec'
o' the sang,
An' when tae them that's far awa'
Ye're writin' ance again,
Jist gie them a' the news ye can
O' oor gran' new Railway train.

An' we'll wish guid luck tae Campbeltown
An may she ever gain,
A routh o' blessings choice an' guid
Frae this Railway o' oor ain.

C.M.

Acknowledgements

This book has not been written from personal recollection and I have been entirely dependent on those who were able to be there when the c & m was running, and have passed on their memories. The specialist knowledge that a railway enthusiast acquires plus a training in locomotive engineering have enabled me to see the old railway through their eyes, as the modern observer would have liked to.

The people of Kintyre have made this book possible, in particular Duncan Colville of Machrihanish who, now in his 80s, has seen the railway at the foot of his garden come and go. Duncan is a keen antiquarian and very little has happened in Dalriada over the last 4,000 years that he doesn't know about. Duncan Colville and the Rev Father Webb combined with D. M. Seaman, the last manager of the mine, to write a manuscript chronicle of coal mining in Kintyre, and this I have freely drawn upon for the chapter on the Campbeltown coalfield.

I have had the good fortune to meet several of the people who worked the railway: driver Jimmy Ramsay, fitter Willie Butters and the superintendent's son Stephen McCabe, all of whom have now passed on. On a happier note, Margaret o' the Train, conductress Margaret Leyden is still very much with us and enjoys a part-time occupation in the creamery, where she has worked since the railway closed.

Although an 'incomer', the Rev John Cormack has been of great help in ferreting information from his parishioners and acting as site agent.

Of the Campbeltown folk, I would like to thank W. Anderson, A. B. Watson, Andrew Cunningham, Mrs Stevenson,

Mrs Maclean (daughter of driver David Lindsay), Mrs N. Wylie
of Machrihanish and a host of others.

The photographs have been credited as far as possible to
those people who are the earliest holders of these pictures.
Should anyone believe he has a prior claim on them, I
apologise.

The sketches in the book were prepared by Fraser Cameron,
who brought his freehand skill as an architect to the rescue of
the author who had been tied too long to the discipline of the
engineer's T square.

The locomotive builders, Andrew Barclay Sons & Co and the
Hunslet Engine Co (successors to Kerr Stuart) generously
supplied information, arrangement drawings and photographs
as did the carriage builders R. Y. Pickering & Co.

James N. Connel Ltd supplied information about the disposal
of the railway.

Vic Goldberg deserves special mention for taking on the task
of sifting through the Chancery records in London and extract-
ing much useful material. Thanks must also go to His Grace,
the Duke of Argyll for giving access to his papers. G. R.
Barbour of the Scottish Records Office assisted in digging out
material and the Campbeltown free library threw open its
doors. The Glasgow Museum of Transport also contributed and
the *Campbeltown Courier* allowed me access to its files.

Of the railway fraternity I must thank Don Boreham, Mike
Hynd, the late George Dott, Ken Melvin, J. F. McEwan, George
Train, Daniel Morrison, P. D. Hancock, Fred Plant, Graham
Langmuir, and A. Fraser.

Finally my undying gratitude goes to my wife Nette for
putting up with all this nonsense, bringing our children up in
a house full of railway and typing this manuscript.

K

Bibliography

Railway Magazine :   1906   page 348, page 390
                        1929   page 21
                        1931   page 31
                        1934   page 79
                        1936   page 25
                        1955   page 660
                        1962   page 510
Locomotive Magazine : 15.6.06   Six-coupled tank locomotive
                     15.10.06   Description of railway
S L S Journal :   August 1948, Article on C & M L R
N C B Coal Magazine : 1952, Coal again from Kintyre
Buses Magazine :   3/69, Buses of Kintyre
L N E R Magazine :   4/32, Article on C & M L R
Smith's Illustrated Views of Campbeltown
Campbeltown Festival Book
History of Campbeltown Coalfield, unpublished ms by Messrs
    Seaman, Webb & Colville
Narrow Gauge Album, P. B. Whitehouse : Chapter 13
Paper on Proposed G & S W R Lines in Kintyre by R. Stirling &
    I. Gillespie, G & S W society
Scottish Field : Sept 1952, Article on Ardkinglas railway by
    A. Macartney
Machrihanish S W R I, Village History Book 1966
8 mm movie film, Campbeltown & Machrihanish Light Rail-
    way by Fraser Cameron
The Campbeltown Colliery & Light Railway, 1902, paper by
    T. Lindsay Galloway

The files of : —
    The Campbeltown Courier 1876-1969

Argyllshire Leader 1929-1934
Argyllshire Herald 1863-1917

Some previous work by the author: —
Model Railway Constructor

October	1953	Drawings, description and photograph of the carriages
November	1953	Drawings, description and photographs of locomotive *Argyll* and C & M L R crest
August	1955	Description and photographs of locomotives *Princess* and *Chevalier*
December	1955	Drawing, description and photograph of locomotive *Princess*
July	1956	Drawings, description and photograph of locomotive *Chevalier*
September	1969	Illustrated article describing the author's exhibition model of Campbeltown

Campbeltown Courier

9 July 1959	serialised: Complete history of the
16 July 1959	Campbeltown & Machrihanish Light Rail-
23 July 1959	way
30 July 1959	

Glossary of Scots Terms

a'	all
aboot	about
ain	own
aither	either
ance	once
ane	one
auld	old
Auld Nick	the Devil
awa	away
bannock	oatcake
bawbee	halfpenny
bickering	quarrelling
bing (coal)	(coal) slag heap
birl	rotate rapidly
blawin	blowing
blaze	type of gravel extracted with coal
bonnie	beautiful
brae	hill
braw	beautiful
coup	tip
dae	do
doon	down
doots	doubts
dram (of whisky)	obsolete liquid measure approx. fifth of a gill
dross	small coal
dyke	wall

falk	folk
frae	from
frien	friend
fricht	fright
gau'n	going
gie	give
gin (horse)	(horse) driven wheel
gite	mad
gaabert	a barge
guid	good
hae	have
hame	home
heid	head
hinner	hinder
hum and haw	argue
hurl	ride
hutch	small colliery wagon
jaunt	excursion
jist	just
ken	know
laddie	a boy
lang	long
lie	railway siding
loch	lake
mair	more
maist	most
maun	must
micht	might
nae	no
noo	now

ony	any
ower	over
oot	out
prood	proud
provost	mayor
puffer (marine)	small coasting vessel
rake	train of wagons
rankle	irritate
ree	depot
roon	round
routh	round
sae	so
sang	song
saut	salt
Sassenach	English
sate	seat
screeve	to scrape causing a high pitched squeal
shoogle	shake
sich	such
sicht	sight
speer	ask
stannin	standing
stob	short post
tae	too
tak	take
toon	town
wad	would
wee	little
weel	well
wrack	wreck

Index